the Back in the Swing cookbook

Recipes for Eating and Living Well
Every Day After Breast Cancer

the Back in the Swing cookbook

Barbara C. Unell and Judith Fertig

Foreword by Rachel S. Beller, MS, RD

Photography by Sara Remington

**Andrews McMeel
Publishing, LLC**
Kansas City • Sydney • London

Andrews McMeel Publishing, LLC
an Andrews McMeel Universal company
1130 Walnut Street
Kansas City, Missouri 64106

www.andrewsmcmeel.com

12 13 14 15 16 SDB 10 9 8 7 6 5 4 3 2 1

ISBN: 978-1-4494-1832-8

Library of Congress Control Number:
2011944354

www.backintheswing.org

The authors of *The Back in the Swing Cookbook* have made every effort to provide information that is accurate and complete as of the date of publication. This book is intended for general informational purposes only, and not as personal medical advice, medical opinion, diagnosis or treatment. The words "woman" and "she" are used when referring to "breast cancer survivor" because the majority of breast cancer diagnoses involve women. The authors of this book acknowledge that men can and do receive breast cancer diagnoses, and that both men and women are the audience for the information of this book.

Book Design: Diane Marsh
Food Photography: Sara Remington
Food Stylist: Erin Quon
Prop Stylist: Christine Wolheim
Artwork: Julie Barnes/iStockphoto.com
All other photos courtesy of iStockphoto.com

If you want to build a ship,
don't drum up the men to gather wood,
divide the work, and give orders.
Instead, teach them to yearn
for the vast and endless sea.

~Antoine de Saint-Exupéry

This book is dedicated to the thousands of brave believers who gave birth to the grassroots nonprofit organization Back in the Swing USA, turning the unthinkable into the inevitable through sheer determination, hard work, a commitment to the greater good, and daring to dream.

Contents

Foreword

To my good fortune, I have a decade's worth of experience as Director of Nutritional Oncology Research & Counseling at leading cancer institutes where I have personally experienced, in both the research and outpatient settings, what women have to go through from cancer diagnosis to treatment and beyond. It was in the post treatment phase where I witnessed the greatest calling for nutritional support.

Although difficult to describe, it was the determined look in patients' eyes that instilled in me an intense passion to assist them in their time of greatest need. I realized long ago that I had to take a proactive stance in the quest of translating scientific research into shopping cart solutions to help oncology patients maximize their healthy lifestyle, while simultaneously helping to prevent recurrence. While working on one of the largest clinical trials ever designed to study prevention of breast cancer through dietary modifications, I saw women try all sorts of remedies that were far from evidence-based.

Many times they would bring as many as 20 bottles and line them up on my desk—"promised cures"—in the hopes of preventing recurrence of their disease. This further ignited the fire in me to present an evidence-based approach that was sustainable.

Today, as President and Founder of the Beller Nutritional Institute, I realize that the key to success in counseling such individuals is to separate the credible research from the hype, and develop a realistic and long-lasting nutritional action plan, a plan that people can understand, own, and take with them back to the busy lives they knew before the "C" word entered their world. The bottom line is that it's about being able to follow it for LIFE!

For me, the secret for both my family and patients is to keep things simple and practical with the ultimate goal of helping individuals feel like they can GET GOING NOW! This is precisely why I believe in the long-term goal that underlies the mission of Back in the Swing USA and this book. In this book, all the research is done, from foods to eat and recipes to prepare . . . to options to get you moving and ways to feel good every day. As a firm believer in the power of food, I decided to go beyond the counseling I provide at the Beller Nutritional Institute and share my message on a larger scale. I'm currently the nutritionist for NBC's *The Biggest Loser*, and serve as nutrition expert for *The Dr. Oz Show*, *Good Morning America*, *Today*, *Glamour* magazine, and numerous other national and international media outlets. In addition, I am a spokesperson for the American Cancer Society. These venues all allow for a larger platform to share the critical role nutrition and weight loss play in cancer prevention. Working with breast cancer patients who are in the public eye ("celebrities") is rewarding, as well, since I also collaborate with them to increase awareness for the cause.

It is my dream, as well as that of Back in the Swing USA, to make this information not only delicious to look at but tangible and easy to use, wherever you live, work, and play. *The Back in the Swing Cookbook* takes all of the information you have and haven't heard, which many in the medical world know but often don't pass on to consumers, and molds it into practical and tasty solutions. This book is singularly unique in that it highlights the pathway to achieve the delicate balance of health, happiness, and long-term wellness. EMPOWER YOURSELF!

Rachel S. Beller, MS, RD
Founder, Beller Nutritional Institute, LLC
bellernutrition.com

Introduction: Back in the Swing Basics

I keep the telephone of my mind
open to peace, harmony, health, love
and abundance. Then whenever doubt,
anxiety or fear try to call me, they keep
getting a busy signal—and soon
they'll forget my number.

~Edith Armstrong

Everyone has a story about a moment in time that changed the course of her life. Indeed, the story of Back in the Swing USA began with one of those moments.

It was a hot Wednesday afternoon in August 1998 when I finished my last radiation treatment for breast cancer. I just naturally assumed that I would get the follow-up care at my cancer center clinic to "put me back together again." I thought that the clinic would provide that care or direct me to those who do, as would a doctor after you get your leg set when it's broken. Routine stuff to get me "back in the swing," as I put it, and help me recover from the side effects of the surgery, chemotherapy, and radiation treatments.

I also just assumed that the personalized medical care that I was getting would continue in some sort of "after-care" posttreatment plan, giving me the prescriptions that I needed to prevent or end the physical side effects, such as:

damage to my heart, fatigue and joint pain from chemotherapy; hot flashes and dry skin from medication; skin damage from radiation; lymphedema from surgery; weakening of my immune system; and bone density loss from all of the above, just to name a few. Again, these routine side effects were known as the "normal," predictable aftermath of the experience, based on my particular primary cancer treatment.

But instead of giving me a plan to put me "back in the swing," my cancer clinic gave me my "walking papers."

"Come back in three months for a follow-up visit and scans," I was told when I had finished my last treatment.

"So what do I do on, well, tonight, or tomorrow, or next Thursday?" I innocently asked. "And how about Friday and Saturday, and the rest of every week until then? How do I improve and protect my health and reduce the risk of cancer recurrence . . . how do I get back in the swing?"

The silence of my health care team spoke volumes. These nationally recognized medical professionals had cared for me to this point but didn't address the effects of the treatment that they had given me. It was if they were pushing me off some sort of cliff, without a parachute of any kind. These people knew what they had done to me, so to speak, and knew about my recent medical history, but it was standard care at that time not to treat anything other than the cancer.

It just didn't make any sense to me: the people who knew best what had caused the new medical issues I was experiencing (weight gain, lymph-

edema, joint pain, muscle aches, bone loss, fatigue, sleeplessness, anxiety, and hot flashes, just to name a few) were not offering any plan to help me recover from them.

Where can I go to receive my personalized, comprehensive medical instructions for getting back in the swing of my life? I asked myself. *And would it be possible for every breast cancer survivor to be able to do so, regardless of where she received her primary treatment?*

A DREAM COMES TRUE

The rest, as the cliché goes, is history.

Along with a team of passionate, fun-loving, dedicated volunteers, I founded the grassroots, nonprofit organization Back in the Swing USA® in 2000 to fill the void in patients having access to personalized, comprehensive clinical breast cancer survivorship health care, education, and medical research.

Our name is our mission. Back in the Swing points consumers and their physicians to the one universal reason that every person with a diagnosis of cancer chooses to get treatment, why she goes to the doctor, and why she suffers the surgeries and insults to her mind and her body: *To get back in the swing of life, physically, emotionally, and spiritually, for the rest of her life.*

"Back in the swing of life" is where every woman wants to be the moment after she is diagnosed . . . and where she wants to be every day thereafter. So why not encourage— through grassroots education, awareness, and fundraising—achieving that goal after experiencing breast cancer? I asked myself.

Therefore, Back in the Swing's mission is to focus its work on the one area in the continuum of cancer care that represents the end goal of treatment: *To improve and protect our health, and prevent cancer recurrence.*

- One of the first achievements of Back in the Swing was to fund and help launch the Breast Cancer Survivorship Center (BCSC) at The University of Kansas Cancer Center, in Westwood, Kansas (nearby Kansas City, Missouri). The BCSC has continued to be a template for other cancer centers and community hospitals, as well as oncology nurses, in how to build evidence-based, comprehensive programs and clinics in breast cancer survivorship. (See page 240 for more on survivorship centers and programs.)

"The gold standard of comprehensive survivorship care," according to Jennifer Klemp, PhD, MPH, managing director of the Breast Cancer Survivorship Center at the University of Kansas Cancer Center, "is to provide each person with personalized, evidence-based recommendations, to empower her to play an active role in her post-treatment care, and to assure her that she has a team she can depend on.

"It is understandable that many survivors report feeling a loss of control after a diagnosis of breast cancer. So a cancer survivorship team can help survivors regain that control by providing each person with education and strategies, within a medical framework, to prevent or manage the physical and emotional effects of her diagnosis and treatment."

- Today, interest in this field has gathered steam since the 2005 release of the book *From Cancer Patient to Cancer Survivor . . . Lost in Transition*, by the Institute of Medicine and National Research Council, and the launch of the groundbreaking Breast Cancer Survivorship Center at the University of Kansas Cancer Center in 2007. Hospital-based programs in cancer survivorship, along with the education of oncology nurses, physicians, nutritionists, exercise physiologists, rehabilitation specialists, genetic counselors, social workers, and patient navigators across the country, have made survivorship clinical care a growing movement in health care.

In 2012, The Commission on Cancer of the American College of Surgeons developed new program standards for accreditation that are, according to the chair of the Commission on Cancer, Stephen Edge, MD, FACS, "much more than a defined structure of clinical treatment," including a survivorship care plan that documents care received and seeks to improve cancer survivors' quality of life, as well as a coordination of care among many medical disciplines ranging from primary care providers to specialists in all oncology disciplines, such as nursing, social work, genetics, nutrition, rehabilitation, and others.

"Integrating this extra layer of support alongside curative treatment is essential to reduce suffering and improve quality of life for cancer patients and their loved ones," says

Otis W. Brawley, MD, chief medical officer of the American Cancer Society, in an August 2011 news release from the Commission on Cancer of the American College of Surgeons. "Cancer patients who seek care at Commission on Cancer–accredited facilities will benefit from interdisciplinary teams who focus on relieving symptoms, pain, and stress, and can help coordinate communication among the patients, their families, and their medical team."

My visits with Patty Ganz, MD, one of the pioneers in breast cancer survivorship research at the Jonsson Comprehensive Cancer Center at UCLA, and Carol Fabian, MD, medical director of the Breast Cancer Prevention and Survivorship Centers at the University of Kansas Cancer Center, both early advisers to Back in the Swing USA, encouraged my colleagues and me to sally forward in our grassroots work to spread the message to consumers about the powerful effects of cancer treatment and prevention therapies, and the need for appreciating these challenges, particularly the impact of nutrition and exercise for each individual's physical and mental health. They and all of us are part of those seeing the dream of Back in the Swing—breast cancer survivorship clinical care as a right, not a privilege—coming true in the twenty-first century.

Barbara C. Unell
February 2012

HOW *THE BACK IN THE SWING COOKBOOK* WAS BORN

"Interdisciplinary teams" can coordinate communication and lead to better health, notes Dr. Otis Brawley of the American Cancer Society. The same holds true for our interdisciplinary team of a foodie and a journalist as coauthors of this book. Exactly what happened when food person, Judith, and journalist, Barbara, discovered that we were on the same wavelength about making every day count, finding joy and meaning in the little things. Together, we wrote this book that reflects the interdisciplinary way we live our lives: We think about what we're going to have for dinner while simultaneously tightening our abs, appreciating a sunset on the horizon as we cruise the roadways, and telling a story to a friend on our cell phone about a new recipe for guacamole!

In addition to making a fun-loving writing team, both of us are self-proclaimed, experienced multitaskers: Judith has authored cookbooks on topics ranging from bread to barbecue, and Barbara has authored parenting books, launched magazines, and founded health and educational programs to help families make positive lifestyle and parenting choices. In that same spirit of collaboration and respect for grassroots, responsive problem solving, Barbara founded the national nonprofit Back in the Swing USA, a grassroots, nonprofit organization solely focused on supporting clinical breast cancer survivorship care, education, and medical research to improve and protect everyone's health and prevent breast cancer.

We bring you—home cooks and novices, health buffs and skeptics—to the table with us, always mindful of the impact of our words on your body, mind, and spirit.

This friendly road map to creating your own definition of eating and living well each day is the book that Barbara was looking for when she was told that she had breast cancer. It would have been impossible to write this book then, however, for one simple reason: Evidence-based recommendations for creating and sustaining a daily "back in the swing" lifestyle and environment were not part of the recommended standard of care for every cancer survivor until the twenty-first century. So now, for the first time in one beautiful place, these recommendations are yours to savor every day.

In these friendly, smart, and satisfying daily recipes for living the good life, you can easily digest what researchers have discovered about 1) genetics, 2) lifestyle choices, 3) the environment, and 4) the influence of all three. Many of the pages introduce you to unique, delicious, and good-for-you food and drink. And many of the pages are filled with information and inspiration that sometimes relate to a recipe on the neighboring pages and often are just tidbits to savor in no particular order:

WHO KNEW? Q & A format of empowering facts explains why the unprocessed foods in each recipe provide so much goodness.

WOULD SOMEONE JUST TELL ME . . . Reports contributed by Katherine Harvey, MS, RD, on the impact of nutrition and lifestyle on primary and secondary cancer prevention, as well as women's health issues and emotional eating.

PROFESSOR POSITIVE Summaries on the evidence-based connections between our emotions and physical and psychological health, contributed by Sarah Pressman, PhD, Beatrice Wright Assistant Professor in the Department of Psychology at the University of Kansas in Lawrence, Kansas. Dr. Pressman's academic research examines the influence of psychosocial factors on physiological and health outcomes, with a focus on how positive psychological factors "get under the skin" to impact illness, disease, and mortality.

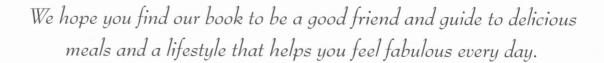

We hope you find our book to be a good friend and guide to delicious meals and a lifestyle that helps you feel fabulous every day.

I KNEW I WAS BACK IN THE SWING WHEN . . . Statements written by breast cancer survivors who finished this sentence on Back in the Swing surveys of survivors in 2011. "On the upswing" sections are also gathered from these surveys and express real-life examples of ways to find joy and humor in the moment and the greater good in life's experiences. Each demonstrates the power of social support in avoiding dwelling on negative thoughts and stimulating healthy brain chemicals by opening your mind to new possibilities.

TREAT OF THE DAY Prescriptions for enjoying the beauty and serenity of sunshine (don't forget the sunscreen!), entertainment, rest, and relaxation to help keep your body, mind, and spirit functioning at their optimum level.

DID YOU HEAR THE NEWS? Scientific research that has led to lifestyle recommendations to help prevent, or reduce the impact of, weight gain, bone loss, cardio-toxicity, fatigue, joint pain, depression, and anxiety, as well as other predictable and treatable common side effects of chemotherapy, radiation, and surgery.

ENERGY BALANCE AND CALORIES OUT Practical ways to balance "calories in" through food choices and "calories out" through exercises that get you moving every day—walking, aerobics, yoga, running, weight-resistance, and bicycling, for example. A balanced lifestyle also strengthens your bones, heart, and immune function.

Our advice? Read, reread, repeat! Find something salty, if you're in the mood to be awakened. Or experiment with one of our calming exercises or meditations, to enjoy along with a cup of tea. When you're feeling adventurous, strap on your apron and take a recipe that you've never tried before for a ride. And reading an essay about nature just might be what gets you cooking on a certain day, when feeling connected to your body, mind, and spirit is in order. These recipes are yours to savor as their style fits your life. They provide the comforting energy, serenity, possibility, and perspective on living the good life.

Barbara C. Unell
Judith Fertig
February 2012

The Back in the Swing Cookbook
Shopping Cart

Each of us has a different reason for wanting to know nutritional information. For some, it's because we are trying to keep a certain number of calories as our daily food count; for others, eating low-sodium food fits the bill. Still others are, well, just curious. We have purposely not advised you about following certain calorie, fat, carbohydrate, sodium, or fiber restrictions; we suggest that you consult with your health care practitioner about the recommended nutrition you need to gain, lose, or maintain your optimum weight, as well as to create the healthy-for-you levels of certain nutrients for improving and protecting your blood, bones, and heart, for example. We provide the back-to-basics canvas here, and you're the artist, using these four easy brushstrokes proven to paint colorful dishes each day: *evidence-based; lean-protein; low-fat; and plant-based recipes for the good life.*

1   EVIDENCE-BASED

We love the way Rachel Beller, MS, RD, the founder of the Beller Nutritional Institute, recommends a common sense approach to what we eat, an approach that we share throughout our book. She notes: "While factors such as age, environment, gender and genetics cannot be controlled, we all possess the power to choose what we eat. Establishing a solid nutritional system that focuses on natural, whole foods is the key to optimum wellness."

These key ingredients are listed in **boldface** type in each recipe. They can be found on several lists of the most nutritious foods that scientific research has demonstrated contribute to optimum health. We also chose the recipes for their flavor and easy-to-fix qualities, making them as good for our bodies and mind, as well as our senses!

If the recipe makes four servings, the nutrition information is for one-fourth of the total recipe. The six categories of nutrients included are in alignment with what you would find on a typical nutrition label on most food products. Katherine Harvey, MS, RD, and her team at the university of Kansas used the University of Minnesota's Nutrition Data System for Research (NDSR) to analyze the recipes; spices were not included in this analyses, nor were the alternatives, substitutions, garnishes, or "to taste" suggestions given for certain ingredients. Substitutions or "to taste" amounts could alter the nutritional results given for the recipe. (You knew that already, but we had to say it!)

Back in the Swing Key Foods

OILS
Canola oil
Grapeseed oil
Olive oil

HERBS/SPICES
Basil
Cinnamon
Garlic
Ginger, plain or pickled
Italian parsley
Lavender
Nutmeg
Oregano
Rosemary
Saffron
Thyme
Turmeric

CANNED GOODS
Black beans
Garbanzo beans (chickpeas)
Pumpkin puree (not seasoned pie filling)
Roasted red peppers
Tahini (sesame paste)
Tomato products
Tuna in olive oil
Vegetable broth

NUTS/SEEDS
Cashews
Edamame
Flaxseed
Pine nuts
Sesame seeds
Walnuts

TEA BLENDS
Ginseng tea
Green tea
Lavender tea
Licorice root tea

DRY GOODS
Chiles (Jalapeño)
Dark chocolate
Cocoa powder
Coffee
Dried beans
Fruits
Nori (dried packaged seaweed)
Oats
Pasta
Quinoa
Rice

FRUITS/VEGETABLES
Apples
Artichokes
Asparagus
Bananas
Bell peppers
Berries
Broccoli
Cabbage
Cherries
Cranberries
Endive
Fresh greens
Juices
Kale
Onion
Peaches
Pineapple
Pomegranate
Red grapes
Root vegetables
Squash
Sweet potatoes
Tomatoes

SWEETENERS
Agave nectar
Brown sugar
Honey
Maple syrup
Sorghum

LEAN PROTEINS
Beans, dried or canned, such as black, cannelli, garbanzo, navy, pinto, or other shelling beans
Bean and vegetable-based protein such as falafel, Seitan, tempeh, tofu
Beef, lean cuts or de-fatted after cooking
Chicken and turkey
Dairy, lower fat or hard grating cheeses such as Parmesan
Eggs
Fish, especially halibut, salmon, and tuna
Shrimp

REFRIGERATED
Almond milk
Eggs
Greek yogurt
Hard grating cheeses
Milk
Miso

2 LEAN-PROTEIN

Every cell in our bodies is made of protein, and protein is also used to build bones, muscles, cartilage, skin, and blood; to repair tissues; and to make enzymes, hormones, and other body chemicals. Protein can also help with Energy Balance because of its satiating properties. Including a small amount of lean protein in all snacks and meals can help you stay full longer. So, we're high on lean protein.

The trick is to get more protein from better food sources. We have included lean meats, beans, eggs, whole grains, and vegetable proteins in our recipes for this very reason. A 2 to 3-ounce serving of meat, chicken, or fish compares in size to a deck of cards; 1 cup of beans counts as 2 ounces of lean protein.

3 LOW-FAT

A high-fat diet has been associated with a higher body mass index (BMI), and a higher BMI is associated with an increase in breast cancer risk, according to the *National Cancer Institute Fact Sheet on Obesity and Cancer*.

A report on the Women's Intervention Nutrition Study (WINS), sponsored by the National Cancer Institute, appeared in the December 20, 2006, issue of the *Journal of the National Cancer Institute*. Researchers found that postmenopausal women who ate a low-fat diet were less likely to get a recurrence of breast cancer than those who ate a standard diet. This is the first time a large, randomized clinical trial has shown that a low-fat diet can reduce the chance of breast cancer coming back.

The WINS Study was a large-prospective, randomized phase III study to investigate whether a low-fat diet could reduce breast cancer recurrence rates in postmenopausal women who had been treated for early-stage breast cancer. Postmenopausal women were chosen because they tend to have less variability in their types of breast cancer than premenopausal women.

From 1994 to 2001, the study enrolled 2,437 women who in the previous year had had breast cancer surgery followed by therapy appropriate to their particular cancer. The women, whose average age was 62, were randomly assigned to one of two dietary groups. One group was asked to follow their standard diet. Women in this group met with a nutritional counselor periodically but were not urged to change their diet, which

To Soy or Not to Soy?

According to Frank Hu, MD, PhD, professor of nutrition and epidemiology at Harvard School of Public Health, meats and many plant-based foods, such as soy, can provide equal amounts of protein.

But here's the catch: Soy foods are a major source of phytoestrogens called isoflavones. Although many studies have found soy foods to be protective against cancer, previous research studies have suggested that soy's isoflavones fuel breast cancer cell growth and possibly interfere with treatment. And a 2011 study reported research demonstrating that soy foods "appear" to be safe, in small amounts, for breast cancer survivors.

It is important to look at the details of scientific reports when using the data for decision making. As mentioned, "eating *small* [our emphasis] amounts of dietary soy may be safe for breast cancer

survivors," concludes a March 2011 study published in *Cancer Epidemiology, Biomarkers & Prevention*. In this study, researchers followed over 3,000 breast cancer survivors for a median of approximately 7 years. When comparing those survivors in the study who had high soy/isoflavone intake (about ½ cup of soy milk or 2 ounces of tofu per day) with those who had the lowest (little to no reported intake), there was no significant difference in cancer recurrence or death, either alone or in combination with tamoxifen treatment.

This study did not evaluate the highest amounts of intake possible, such as the amount found in a high protein shake or energy bar, which contain more than 10 grams each. The authors report that the highest intake of those in the study was 16.3mg/day, which is significantly less than what the soy protein intake would be if someone's daily diet included ½ cup soymilk, 2 ounces of tofu, a soy protein bar, and a shake.

The jury is still out, we have concluded, on the impact of high–soy protein foods. Therefore, check with your health practitioner on balancing your sources of protein, which may include a small amount of dietary soy/isoflavone.

Note: Soy fillers are additives in many processed foods, and the amounts are not normally listed on the label. So it is often challenging to determine the amount of soy you actually eat on any given day.

contained an average of about 51 grams of fat a day (about 40 percent of total calories from fat).

After a median of five years of follow-up, breast cancer had come back in 9.8 percent of the women on the low-fat diet and 12.4 percent of those on the standard diet. This amounted to a 24 percent reduction in the risk of recurrence for the women on the low-fat diet.

The largest risk reduction, 42 percent, was seen among women on the low-fat diet whose tumors did not respond to the presence of the hormone estrogen. Breast cancer that doesn't respond to estrogen is called estrogen receptor negative (ER-negative). Postmenopausal women whose tumors do respond to estrogen are candidates for antiestrogen drugs such as tamoxifen or an aromatase inhibitor (such as arimidex, letrozole, and aromasin), which help reduce the risk of recurrence.

These results cannot prove that the low-fat diet was responsible for the lower rate of recurrence in the women assigned to that group. Other factors, including the modest weight loss seen in the low-fat group or increased consumption of fruit and vegetables, may have contributed to the outcome. But the take-home message is that a lower-fat diet may be beneficial in reducing our breast cancer risk.

In another study at Harvard University, researchers recently conducted a prospective analysis of 90,655 premenopausal women, ages 26 to 46, enrolled in the Nurses' Health Study II since 1989, and determined that intake of animal fat, especially from red meat and high-fat dairy products, during premenopausal years is associated with

an increased risk of breast cancer. Increased risk was not associated with vegetable fats.

In addition, researchers at the Ontario Cancer Institute conducted a meta-analysis of all the case-control and cohort studies published up to July 2003 that studied dietary fat, fat-containing foods, and breast cancer risk. Case-control and cohort study analyses yielded similar risk results, with a high total fat intake associated with increased breast cancer risk. Significant relative risks for meat and saturated fat intake also were noted, with high meat intake increasing cancer risk by 17 percent and high saturated fat intake increasing cancer risk by 19 percent.

4 PLANT-BASED

The plant-based recipes here follow the lead of laboratory research that suggests "eating vegetables, fruits, whole grains and beans will protect against cancer," as noted by the American Institute for Cancer Research (AICR.org).

Carrying excess body fat is implicated in the development of cancer, as noted here. The AICR says: "Eating a predominantly plant-based diet can help prevent weight gain and protect against those cancers whose risk is convincingly increased by higher body fat (cancers of the colorectum, esophagus, endometrium, pancreas, kidney, and breast in postmenopausal women)."

The AICR recommends that "at least ⅔ of your plate should be filled with vegetables, fruit, whole grains and beans"—another reason why this book is chock full of recipes that include these ingredients, each of which is in **boldface** in the ingredients list for each recipe.

On the website of Stand Up to Cancer (Standup2cancer.org), an article by Cat Vasko notes: "William Li, MD, president and medical director [of the Angiogenesis Foundation] (angio.org), says, 'Drugs are prescribed by doctors, but what happens in between the times you see your doctor? There has been a huge gap in the research when it comes to arming patients with their own tools. We want to shift the paradigm away from relying only on the doctor by putting information in the hands of the patient, and a major part of that shift is changing how we think about food.'"

But Dr. Li, doesn't want to focus on what should be removed from our diets; instead, he wants to look at what are the naturally occurring foods we can add to our diets to boost our bodies' defenses.

Rachel Beller, MS, RD, agrees: "Emerging laboratory research has shown that certain foods can potentially provide the body with cancer-fighting nutrients, which may reduce the risk of breast cancer. And, some of the most important of these cancer-fighting foods can be found in the produce section of your local supermarket."

Recipe for Living Well

The easy answer to not getting crazy about food's "good or bad" properties is to realize that weight gain and higher body fat can be a result of not only the actual makeup of the food and drink but also the portions we eat. (See page xxiv for more on serving size.) Here's the "perfect storm" in our culture that promotes weight gain, according to Katherine Harvey, MS, RD:

- We have more access to food than ever before. Around every corner is a restaurant, vending machine, coffee shop, and candy dish;

- Advances in technology have enabled us to become sedentary—we get around everywhere in our cars, sit behind computers all day, and order things online rather than physically shopping for them; and

- Despite the efficiency of our advances, we are busier than ever.

To avoid getting in the path of this perfect storm:

1   BECOME AWARE.
First, pay attention to all of the exposure you have to food, including advertisements, places to buy it, sights, sounds, smells. You will quickly notice that food stimuli are everywhere, and you are being exposed to subliminal messages constantly. As you become aware of your exposure, become mindful of your portion sizes, particularly at restaurants. Societal norms imply that we should routinely eat large amounts of food. Often the food served to you is enough for three or four people (see Serving Sizes, page xxiv).

Also, bring awareness to your body and its ways of communicating with you. Do you feel hunger in your stomach? Your head? Your chest? Is your hunger physical or mental? Then become aware of how you feel after you have eaten. If you clean your plate, how do you feel afterward? What happens if you leave a couple of bites or save half for later? How do you feel?

2   TAKE CONTROL.

What if you eat only a cup of your pasta and feel almost full, possibly with room for a piece of fine chocolate or a cup of coffee to finish off the meal and leave you feeling satisfied but not stuffed? This would likely be a much more pleasant experience than eating until you "cannot eat another bite." When you become aware that you are not a mere victim to your surroundings, you can start to take charge of your decisions.

This might mean starting some new habits. Perhaps you pack your own snacks for the day or choose to order soup and an appetizer rather than a full entrée at lunch with your coworkers. Maybe you spend your break time walking around the block or get up thirty minutes early to do some exercise before beginning your day. Making choices that enhance your health and well-being is empowering. Recent research has shown that when you take ownership of your decisions, you are much more likely to stick to them long-term.

3   FIND BALANCE.

Strive for a sense of balance in the time you devote to your work and family life, balance your nutrients, balance cardio with strength exercises, and even try balancing a yoga pose . . . you get the idea.

SERVING SIZES: QUANTITY OVER QUALITY

Serving sizes in many restaurants are bigger now than they have ever been. Many consumers have come to value quantity over quality of food, and the result has been a steady rise in the overweight and obesity rates. Studies have also shown that when we are served larger portions, we eat more.

So how can we estimate portions when we don't have a measuring cup or scale handy? Here are some ways, keeping in mind that hands and fingers come in all sizes!

- 1 cup: a closed fist or cupped hand

- ½ cup of cooked cereal, pasta, rice, vegetable, or canned fruit: a cupcake wrapper

- 3 ounces of meat: the palm of your hand or the size of a deck of cards

- 3 ounces of grilled or baked fish: the size of a checkbook cover

- 1 teaspoon: the tip of your thumb (from the knuckle up)

- 1 ounce of cheese: the size of your thumb (from the palm to the fingertip)

- 1 potato: the size of a computer mouse

"*Life is uncertain.*
Eat dessert first."

~Ernestine Ulmer

CHAPTER ONE
Desserts

Like a Kid Again

"We are always the same age inside."

~Gertrude Stein

We thought about it. And made the big decision. Our first chapter would be desserts, to anticipate the most popular taste—sweet!

The Back in the Swing approach to sugar, just as in all things, is to separate myth from fact. The sweet things in life, including desserts, can fit into healthy eating and everyday lifestyle. Indeed, what is it about desserts that can bring a smile to even the grumpiest adult? Dessert is meant to be lighthearted. Desserts, after all, is the reverse spelling of stressed.

More than any other part of the meal, a favorite dessert instantly takes us back to treasured moments of sweetness, when we were treated to something special. Think birthday cake!

Dessert encourages us to engage our playful side, especially true if we are indulging in a familiar confection with a new twist: a carrot cake cupcake, a chocolate cake with a secret filling, or a frozen yogurt that tastes like cherry cheesecake.

I started to laugh again!

~Cindy Himmelberg, art director

Brambleberry Crisp

A mixture of lemon, spice, and berries with a crunchy topping, this dessert is full of delicious flavor and good-for-you ingredients. Use a fine-rasp grater (such as a microplane) or a nutmeg grater to get the freshest flavor from the nutmeg. This handy metal kitchen tool grates everything from hard cheese and citrus zest to spices. The design features a series of small etched teeth, giving you more control over your grating.

Serves 6 • Prep Time: 5 minutes • Cook Time: 30 to 35 minutes

FILLING

3	cups fresh or thawed frozen **blackberries**, sliced **strawberries**, **blueberries**, and/or pitted sour **cherries**
¼	cup **honey**
1	tablespoon fresh **lemon juice**
1	tablespoon cornstarch
¼	teaspoon freshly grated **nutmeg**
¼	teaspoon ground **cinnamon**

TOPPING

1	tablespoon unsalted butter, at room temperature
1	tablespoon **grapeseed oil** or **canola oil**
¼	cup white whole wheat or regular whole wheat flour
1	tablespoon packed light **brown sugar**
½	teaspoon freshly grated **nutmeg**
½	teaspoon ground **cinnamon**
1½	teaspoons **honey**
½	cup old-fashioned rolled **oats**

1. Preheat the oven to 400°F. Coat a 6-cup soufflé dish or deep baking dish with a small amount of oil or butter.

2. For the filling, combine the berries, honey, lemon juice, cornstarch, nutmeg, and cinnamon in a large bowl and stir gently to blend. Spoon the filling into the prepared dish.

3. For the topping, using the same bowl if you wish, combine the butter, oil, flour, brown sugar, nutmeg, cinnamon, honey, and oats with a wooden spoon until well blended. Drop the mixture by spoonfuls on top of the filling.

4. Bake for 30 to 35 minutes, until browned and bubbling. Let cool on a wire rack for 10 minutes. To serve, spoon the warm crisp onto dessert plates and top with frozen yogurt, if you like.

Calories 176 • Total Fat 5g • Saturated Fat 1.5g
Carbohydrates 27.5g • Protein 2.5g
Dietary Fiber 5g • Sodium 30mg

Are positive emotions positively positive?

Our "Professor Positive," Sarah Pressman, PhD, was the principal investigator in a joint study between the University of Kansas and Gallup, presented in March 2009 at the annual meeting of the American Psychosomatic Society in Chicago. The research investigated whether feelings, such as happiness or sadness, matter to the health of people who have more pressing concerns, including getting enough to eat or finding shelter.

During the study, the researchers analyzed the data from the Gallup World Poll involving more than 150,000 adults. The participants reported their emotions and also answered questions about whether their most basic needs like food, shelter, and personal safety were adequately met.

Results showed that positive emotions, such as happiness and enjoyment, are unmistakably linked to better health, even when taking into account a lack of basic needs. On the other hand, negative emotions, such as worry and sadness, were predictive of worse health. The association between emotions and physical health was more powerful than the connection between health and basic human physical requirements.

Common Myths About *Sweeteners*

MYTH NO. 1: Sugar feeds cancer.

This is not true. Tumors do use glucose (a component of sugar) for fuel, but they do not get it directly from eating sugar. Our body converts all of its stored energy (which comes from carbohydrates, fat, and protein) into glucose when it needs it. Glucose feeds virtually all cells in the body, not just tumor cells. So what's the concern? An excess of high-caloric foods (often those that are also high in fat and sugar) can increase the risk of a high body mass index (BMI) and an elevated insulin level, both of which have been linked to increased cancer risk.

MYTH NO. 2: Artificial sweeteners cause cancer.

All artificial sweeteners are regulated by the U.S. Food and Drug Administration. There is currently no evidence that these substances cause cancer. Some studies using laboratory rats suggest that an artificial sweetener called saccharin is linked to bladder cancer. This same association has never been proven in humans for saccharin or any other artificial sweetener.

MYTH NO. 3: Agave nectar has not been shown to have any health benefits.

Agave nectar is a juice extracted from the agave plant, which is then heated, filtered, and concentrated into a syrup. Some studies have suggested that agave nectar causes a lower insulin response than regular sugar, which may be beneficial. It contains more calories per teaspoon than regular table sugar (20 compared to 15), which is essentially the same as honey. If you like the taste of agave nectar, feel free to use it; but like all things, use in moderation.

MYTH NO. 4: High-fructose corn syrup causes obesity.

High-fructose corn syrup has gotten a bad reputation in recent years. It is sweeter than regular sugar and inexpensive to produce, so the food and beverage industry often uses it as their sweetener of choice because it is cost-effective. However, once in the body, it is processed essentially the same as sugar. Studies have shown that high-fructose corn syrup does not cause obesity any more than sugar. The bigger problem lies in our overall consumption of sweeteners, not necessarily the type. As far as weight gain goes, a calorie is a calorie, no matter where it comes from.

SWEETENER	CALORIES (PER TEASPOON)	POSSIBLE BENEFITS	POSSIBLE CONCERNS
Agave Nectar	20	• Lower insulin response • May contain antioxidants	
Aspartame (NutraSweet, Equal)	13	• Much sweeter than sugar, so very small amounts are needed • Minimal insulin response	
High-Fructose Corn Syrup	18	• Sweeter than sugar so less is needed • Inexpensive	• Elevated consumption in processed foods
Honey	21	• Minimally processed • Contains antioxidants	• Botulism in children <1 year old
Saccharine (Sweet'N Low)	0	• Noncaloric • No insulin response • Does not promote dental cavities	• Early concerns about cancer dismissed
Stevia	0	• Natural, noncaloric • No insulin response	
Sucanat	15	• Minimally processed • May contain antioxidants	
Sucrose (table sugar, white and brown)	15		• Promotes dental cavities
Sugar Alcohols	0-3	• Lower insulin response	• May cause gastrointestinal distress

Pineapple with Blueberry–Ginger Sauce

The topping is so delicious, you'll want to just take a spoonful and savor it all by itself. Use a microplane zester/grater to easily grate the fresh ginger, skin and all. If you like, add a dollop of Greek yogurt.

Serves 4 • Prep Time: 5 Minutes

2 cups fresh or thawed frozen **blueberries**

¼ cup **honey**, **agave nectar**, or **sorghum**

1½ teaspoons freshly grated **ginger**

2 cups fresh **pineapple** rings (or canned, in juice, not syrup)

1 Place the blueberries, honey, and ginger in a food processor or blender fitted with the steel blade and puree until smooth. Serve over fresh pineapple.

Calories 150 • Total Fat 0.5g • Saturated Fat 0g • Carbohydrates 39g
Protein 1g • Dietary Fiber 3g • Sodium 3mg

Sweet Couscous with Dark Chocolate and Dried Fruit

Sandra Boynton, author of *Chocolate: The Consuming Passion*, notes, "Research tells us that 14 out of any 10 individuals like chocolate." This comforting, simple combination of fruits and chocolate is adapted from a recipe by Mark Bittman, noted cookbook author and food columnist for the *New York Times*.

Serves 2 • Prep Time: 5 minutes • Cook Time: 10 minutes

1   cup plain or vanilla-flavored **almond milk**

1   cup uncooked **Power Pilaf** (page 221) or Israeli or pearl couscous

¼   teaspoon almond extract (optional)

2   tablespoons **dark chocolate** chunks or chocolate chips

2   tablespoons chopped dried **cherries**, **cranberries**, **apricots**, or golden **raisins**

1   In a saucepan over medium-high heat, bring the almond milk to a boil and stir in the pilaf. Cover and cook for 10 minutes, or until tender. Fluff with a fork.

2   Stir in the almond extract, if using, chocolate, and dried fruit. Enjoy warm, at room temperature, or cold.

Calories 135 • Total Fat 3.5g • Saturated Fat 2g • Carbohydrates 20.5g Protein 5g • Dietary Fiber 1g • Sodium 55 mg

Get a jump on healthy living!

Some voices—family, friends, doctors, even our own—may tell us, "Don't exercise, take it easy, you've been through so much . . . just rest." But the scientific research tells us to ignore those voices and get moving, even if we've never exercised before.

Many studies show that being overweight at the time of breast cancer diagnosis and weight gain after diagnosis are linked to higher rates of recurrence and lower survival rates. To complicate matters even more is this fact: Treatment can cause weight gain. And we're not talking about a pound or two. In an article in the December 18, 2011, issue of *HUFFPOST Healthy Living*, Dr. Wendy Demark-Wahnefried of the University of Alabama at the Birmingham Department of Nutrition says that in one year, women who received chemotherapy for breast cancer experienced muscle loss and fat gain that was similar to ten years of normal aging. So a forty-five-year-old may find herself with the body type of a fifty-five-year-old.

But wait, the news is good from the research published in the May 25, 2005, issue of the *Journal of the American Medical Association (JAMA)*, which says that physical activity after diagnosis can boost survival rates . . . even modest amounts of exercise. The greatest benefit occurred in women who performed the equivalent of walking three to five hours per week at an average pace. Numbers like these are hard to ignore . . . so try the following recipe to get moving now.

Instant Exercise!

Angie Ford, Jazzercise® Center owner, shares these simple tried-and-true, time-saving ways to fit fitness into your busy life. Remember these daily tasks to make exercise a natural part of your day, every day:

POP IN A DVD. Remember that aerobic means rhythmic or continuous, with an increased heart rate for at least 20 minutes, so find a recipe that takes at least that much time to bake and pop in a good exercise DVD (I love the Jazzercise® "Dancin' Abs" thirty-minute version!).

REMEMBER THE PUNCH LINE. Imagine that you're getting punched in the gut. To exercise your core, hold that feeling for a count of twenty. You can practice this core workout in your car or while standing in the check out line at the grocery store. Stronger core = stronger back = better balance = avoiding falls.

GET TO THE HEART OF THE MATTER. Your heart is a muscle, so you have to exercise it. To do so, you need to get it pumping on a regular basis. Weekend warrior-type stuff doesn't work. Slow and steady wins the race, so consistency is just as important, if not more so, than intensity.

GET SNEAKY. Here are four simple ways to sneak in some fun and practical exercise moments throughout the course of your day:

- Park farther away from the grocery store door.

- Vacuum out your car (use your core muscles when tipping forward to get under seats).

- Take a quick walk with the dog (or neighbor).

- Avoid the elevator and take the stairs.

HYDRATE BEFORE, DURING, AND AFTER EXERCISING. Studies have found that athletes who lose as little as 2 percent of body weight through sweating have a drop in blood volume which can cause the heart to work harder to circulate blood. With this drop in blood volume may come cramps, dizziness, fatigue, heat exhaustion, and stroke. So drink plenty of water.

FUN IS THE MOTIVATOR. If you aren't having fun with your workout, you are less likely to stick with it. Since consistency is the key, it's important to find something that feels joyous and not like a "chore."

WHO KNEW?

Q: Is it okay to use cooking spray when I bake?

A: According to a study published in the *Seattle Post-Intelligencer*, December 20, 2007, even small amounts of the sprays, when heated, released high concentrations of diacetyl, a chemical that can cause serious and even fatal respiratory disease under repeated, long-term exposure. Although manufacturers have since removed products containing diacetyl from the market, some health advocates fear that using aerosol products is still risky since the long-term effects of inhaling the particles and vapors of other artificial ingredients isn't known. Alternatively, an oil-spray pump sold at cookware stores works very similarly to a store-bought version (i.e., Pam) but also has key differences: You can fill the container with any oil of your choice. You manually pump air into the cylinder, which causes an increased internal pressure. Upon pushing the button, the pressure is released and oil is expelled onto the pan or food surface. There is no aerosol or artificial chemicals. This handy tool is a very healthy way of applying small amounts of fresh oil to foods.

Banana, Cinnamon, and Walnut Bundt Cake

If you're a person who shows your love by baking, you'll want to keep this recipe handy. The cake has a lovely cinnamon flavor; serve each slice with a spoonful of the easy dessert sauce, warm or at room temperature.

Serves 12 • Prep Time: 25 minutes • Cook Time: 40 minutes

1¾ cups all-purpose flour, plus more for the pan

¾ cup white whole wheat flour

1¼ teaspoons baking soda

1¼ teaspoons baking powder

½ teaspoon salt

3 large **egg** whites

⅓ cup **honey**, **agave nectar**, or **sorghum**

1 cup **buttermilk**

1 cup mashed **bananas** (about 3 large)

1 teaspoon vanilla extract

FILLING

¼ cup packed dark **brown sugar**

¼ cup granulated sugar

1 tablespoon ground **cinnamon**

¼ teaspoon freshly grated **nutmeg**

¼ cup chopped **walnuts** or pecans, for topping

2 cups **Blueberry-Lavender Sauce**, for serving

1 Preheat the oven to 350°F. Grease and flour a Bundt or tube pan and tap out any excess flour over the sink. Set aside.

2 In a large bowl, combine the all-purpose flour, whole wheat flour, baking soda, baking powder, and salt.

3 In a smaller bowl, beat the egg whites until fluffy with a mixer. Then beat in the sweetener, buttermilk, bananas, and vanilla. With a spatula or large metal spoon, fold the dry ingredients into the banana mixture until you can't see any more flour.

4 For the filling, combine the brown sugar, granulated sugar, cinnamon, and nutmeg in a small bowl.

5 Spoon half the batter into the prepared pan, and sprinkle with the filling. Spoon the remaining batter on top of the filling and smooth with a spatula. Sprinkle the top with walnuts.

6 Bake for 37 to 40 minutes, until a toothpick entered near the center comes out clean. Cool on a wire rack. Invert onto a cake plate and serve with the sauce.

TIP: If you don't have buttermilk, substitute 2 teaspoons fresh lemon juice or vinegar in 1 cup milk. Stir well. Let sit for 5 minutes before using.

Calories 179 • Total Fat 2g • Saturated Fat 0.3g Carbohydrates 26g • Protein 5g • Dietary Fiber 3g Sodium 137mg

Blueberry-Lavender Sauce

Use this versatile sauce for breakfast, lunch, or dinner. It's just as delicious warm over pancakes and waffles as it is at room temperature over yogurt. Warm it up again to serve over frozen yogurt for dessert. Keeps covered in the refrigerator for up to 1 week.

Makes about 2 cups; 2 tablespoons per serving • Prep Time: 5 minutes • Cook Time: 5 minutes

2 cups fresh or thawed frozen **blueberries**

½ teaspoon organic dried **lavender** buds

¼ cup **agave nectar**

2 teaspoons fresh **lemon juice**

1 Combine the blueberries, lavender, and agave nectar in a saucepan over medium-high heat.

2 Cook, stirring, for 5 minutes, or until the blueberries are soft and juicy.

3 Remove from the heat. Add the lemon juice, cover, and let steep for 15 minutes. Serve warm or at room temperature.

Spice Cake with Honeyed Carrot Topping

Cooked in honey until they are deliciously candied, the carrots in the topping make you smile. They're brilliantly colored, all-natural decoration that you know is good for your eyesight, too. But it's the wonderful spice flavor and moist, airy texture of this old-fashioned cake that seals the deal.

Serves 9 • Prep Time: 15 minutes • Cook Time: 30 minutes

CAKE

2   large **eggs**, beaten

½   cup packed **light brown sugar**

¾   cup canned **pumpkin** puree (not seasoned pie filling)

2   tablespoons **molasses**

¾   cup all-purpose flour

1   teaspoon baking powder

1   teaspoon ground **cinnamon**

1   teaspoon ground **ginger**

¼   teaspoon freshly grated **nutmeg**

HONEYED CARROT TOPPING

2   large **carrots**, peeled and coarsely grated

¼   cup **honey**

¼   cup water

2   teaspoons fresh **lemon juice**

1   Preheat the oven to 375°F. Coat a 9-inch square baking pan with a small amount of oil or butter and set aside.

2   For the cake, beat the eggs in a medium bowl with an electric mixer at high speed for about 2 minutes, until pale yellow. Beat in the brown sugar, 1 tablespoon at a time. Beat in the pumpkin and molasses at medium speed, until well blended. Combine the flour, baking powder, cinnamon, ginger, and nutmeg in a bowl. Stir the flour mixture into the batter with a mixing spoon until well blended. Spoon the batter into the prepared pan.

3   Bake for 20 minutes, or until a toothpick inserted into the center comes out clean.

4 For the topping, place the carrots, honey, and water in a small saucepan. Bring to a boil over medium-high heat, then reduce the heat and simmer, stirring occasionally, for 10 minutes, or until the carrots are dark orange and most of the liquid has evaporated. Stir in the lemon juice. Let cool in the pan.

5 To serve, cut the cake into 9 pieces. Use a fork to spread each piece with the topping.

Calories 178 • Total Fat 7g • Saturated Fat 4g
Carbohydrates 21g • Protein 7g
Dietary Fiber 0g • Sodium 152 mg

PROFESSOR POSITIVE
Friends are good medicine.

Extensive research has shown that not only do friends ease your mind, they can lower your physiological responses to stress, as well. In July 2010, researchers from Brigham Young University reviewed 148 studies that tracked the social habits of more than 300,000 people. They found that people who have strong ties to family, friends, or coworkers have a 50 percent lower risk of dying over a given period than those with fewer social connections, according to the journal *Plos Medicine*.

When surveyed by Back in the Swing, breast cancer survivors ranked their friends as one of the most helpful sources of their getting back in the swing.

Poached Cherries with Honey Cream and Fresh Mint

Poaching cherries in cherry-pomegranate juice, instead of a sugary syrup, gives you fantastic flavor and a multitasking boost of vitamins. Look for a cherry-pomegranate juice with no sugar added. Then whip up a delicious cream, sort of a lighter mascarpone, to serve with the cherries.

Serves 4 • Prep Time: 15 minutes • Cook Time: 7 to 10 minutes

1 cup **cherry-pomegranate juice**, such as Old Orchard

1 tablespoon **honey**, **agave nectar**, or **sorghum**

2 cups fresh pitted or thawed frozen sweet **cherries**

1 teaspoon fresh **lemon juice**

2 ounces Neufchâtel cheese, at room temperature

6 ounces nonfat **Greek yogurt**, such as Fage

2 tablespoons clover or wildflower **honey**

Fresh mint sprigs, for garnish

1 Bring the juice and honey to a boil over high heat in a large saucepan. Add the cherries, reduce the heat, and simmer for 7 to 10 minutes, until the cherries are soft and plump. Off-heat, stir in the lemon juice and taste.

2 Combine the cheese, yogurt, and honey in a mixer, blender, or food processor and blend until smooth. Spoon the honey cream into bowls and top with warm cherries. Garnish with mint.

Calories 206 • Total Fat 4g • Saturated Fat 2g • Carbohydrates 51g
Protein 4g • Dietary Fiber 1.5g • Sodium 78 mg

I believe that how you move your body is a reflection of how you move through life.

~Carol LaRue

Throughout life, there is a constant flow of movement and change—calm and chaos, ease and disease, illness and health. Moving our bodies is a great way to practice our flexibility, agility, strength, adaptability, and resiliency to these changes.

I know that moving my body is my healing path. It creates feelings of joy, peace, and a sense of inner connection with myself—in the moment. It clears my mind, energizes and relaxes my body, helps me express my emotions, and lifts and expands my spirit. I even talk better when I am moving! Whether I am dancing, stretching, walking, pumping iron, or breathing deeply and rhythmically, movement feels natural—like coming home to the essential nature of my soul.

The vital, tingling sensations of my body during yoga, core strengthening, brisk or mindful walking, and sensuous meditative or expressive dance trigger immense feelings of gratitude and appreciation for the miracle of my body. Through movement, I feel my body's natural desire for balance, and its ability to shift, change, and heal. Every day I celebrate the present moment of life through moving my body in whatever way it is calling for in this moment. Even moving into stillness—sitting in meditation is a way to move toward and into my center—my home in myself.

It has always been vital for me to spend time close to nature, particularly near water. Mother Earth is such a grand and wise teacher, reminding me of the natural cycle of light and dark, rest and activity, death and rebirth, the renewal through constant change, and the inter connectivity of all beings. Breathing in the musty aroma of the earth in spring, quietly observing a sunset, or walking in the silence of the snow-covered earth fills my entire being with reverence and awe at the inner knowing and natural balance of the universe . . . of the grace in everything . . . of grace *moving* within me.

Carol LaRue is an occupational therapist and the author of *The Art of Self-Health: Creating Well-Being from the Inside Out.*

Brown Sugar and Walnut Meringues with Fresh Strawberries

Piled high in glass compote dishes, these airy meringue cookies and fresh whole strawberries look fabulous on your dinner or buffet table for a help-yourself dessert. When strawberries are not available, the cookies are delicious with Baked Lemon-Spice Apples (page 34). If you like, gently pack the cookies in cellophane bags, tie them with a beautiful ribbon, and give them as gifts from your kitchen.

Makes 36 cookies; serves 12 • Prep Time: 15 minutes • Cook Time: 30 minutes

½ cup **egg** whites (from about 4 large eggs)

¼ teaspoon salt

1 cup packed light **brown sugar**

¼ cup toasted **walnuts**, finely chopped

1 quart fresh **strawberries**

1 Preheat the oven to 300°F. Line 2 baking sheets with parchment paper.

2 With an electric mixer, beat the egg whites and salt on high speed until soft peaks form.

3 Add ½ cup of the brown sugar and continue to beat on high speed until stiff peaks form. Add the remaining sugar, 1 tablespoon at a time, continuing to beat at high speed, until the mixture is stiff and shiny. With a rubber spatula, quickly fold in the walnuts until they're dispersed throughout, but the mixture has not deflated. Drop by tablespoons, about 2 inches apart, onto the prepared pans. Flatten each cookie slightly with the back of a spoon.

4 Bake for about 30 minutes, until golden brown. Let cool. Store the cookies in an airtight container until ready to serve with the strawberries.

TIP: To toast nuts, arrange them on a baking sheet and toast in a 350°F oven for 15 minutes or until lightly browned and fragrant. Let cool, then chop.

Calories 142 • Total Fat 2g • Saturated Fat 0g • Carbohydrates 30g
Protein 2g • Dietary Fiber 1.5g • Sodium 95 mg

Pets get your heart pumping.

Exercise is the focus of this Energy Balance tip: Woman's best friend is so much more than her faithful companion. She's her exercise buddy and social magnet, too.

A March 2011 study at Michigan State University showed that promoting dog ownership and dog walking could help many people become healthier.

Using data from the Michigan Department of Community Health, researchers found that not only did owning and walking a dog affect the amount of walking a person does but also that dog walkers were more active overall. Study coauthor Dr. Mathew Reeves told the *Journal of Physical Activity and Health*: "The findings suggest public health campaigns that promote the responsible ownership of a dog along with the promotion of dog walking may represent a logical opportunity to increase physical activity."

One key to a healthy mind is staying engaged with others. And pet owners have a tendency to want to talk with other pet owners, especially while walking a dog. You have a built-in conversation starter when you take your dog to a dog park for an even greater opportunity to socialize with other owners, while your pet makes new friends, too.

Persian Rice Pudding

This golden rice pudding, flavored with saffron and turmeric, stirs up outrageously unique sweet, wholesome goodness. You can also cook the rice in vanilla-flavored almond milk, so it works for a vegan diet.

Serves 4 • Prep Time: 5 minutes • Cook Time: 30 minutes

2 cups 2% **milk**

¼ cup **honey**, **agave nectar**, or **sorghum**

½ teaspoon **saffron** threads, or 1 teaspoon ground **cinnamon**

⅛ teaspoon ground **turmeric**

¼ teaspoon salt

½ cup long grain white or brown **rice**

¼ cup golden **raisins**, dried **cherries**, **cranberries**, or chopped dried apricots

¼ cup roasted chopped **cashews** or roasted, shelled pistachios, for garnish

1 Bring the milk and sweetener to a simmer over medium-high heat in a large, heavy-bottomed saucepan. Stir in the saffron, turmeric, salt, and rice. Reduce the heat to low, cover, and cook for 20 minutes, stirring occasionally.

2 Stir in the raisins and cook for 10 minutes longer, uncovered, or until the rice is tender, the pudding is thick, and the raisins are plump. Serve topped with the nuts.

Calories 202 • Total Fat 6g • Saturated Fat 2g • Carbohydrates 33.5g
Protein 5.5g • Dietary Fiber 1g • Sodium 235 mg

WHO KNEW?

Q: What is turmeric?

A: It is a food in the same family as ginger. The active ingredient in turmeric is curcumin. Turmeric has been known for over twenty-five hundred years in India, where it was most likely first used as a dye. Long known for its anti-inflammatory properties, recent research has revealed that turmeric may be beneficial in the treatment of many health conditions, from cancer to Alzheimer's disease.

Old-Fashioned Chocolate Pudding with Fresh Berries

We take our chocolate very seriously. The deep, rich flavor of this pudding, adapted from a recipe by our friend Kathleen Leighton, is a new favorite. The little bit of coffee powder accentuates the chocolate, making this truly a masterpiece that will end your love affair with store-bought pudding. Use a fine-rasp grater, such as a microplane, or a nutmeg grater for the wonderful, don't-miss touch of freshly grated nutmeg, or purchase nutmeg already ground for a time-saver.

Serves 8 • Prep Time: 15 minutes • Cook Time: 10 minutes

¼ cup unsweetened **cocoa** powder

¼ cup unsifted cornstarch

½ cup sugar

¼ teaspoon salt

1 tablespoon instant regular or espresso **coffee**

¼ teaspoon freshly grated **nutmeg**

1 large **egg**, at room temperature

2½ cups 2% **milk**

1 tablespoon cold unsalted butter, cut into pieces

⅔ cup semisweet **chocolate** chips

2 teaspoons vanilla extract

1 pint fresh **raspberries** or **strawberries**

1. In a medium saucepan, whisk the cocoa, cornstarch, sugar, salt, coffee, and nutmeg together. In a bowl, whisk the egg and milk together. Pour half of the milk mixture into the dry cocoa mixture and whisk until blended and smooth. Whisk in the remaining milk mixture and use a spatula to get around the perimeter of the pan. Place the saucepan over medium heat and whisk on and off for about 5 minutes, until steam rises from the edges of the pan.

2. Slowly whisk in the butter and chocolate chips without stopping (to avoid lumps) for 4 to 5 minutes, until the pudding starts to thicken and looks smooth. As soon as you see big bubbles rise to the surface, keep whisking for 1 minute longer to finish cooking the cornstarch. Remove from the heat, stir in the vanilla, and set aside to cool. If you don't want a skin to form on the surface, place plastic wrap or oiled parchment paper directly on the pudding.

3. To serve, spoon the pudding into bowls, top with a dollop of Little Black Dress "whipped cream," if you like, and scatter with berries.

Little Black Dress "Whipped Cream"

The French love a dollop of crème fraîche, a thick and tangy cream, on their desserts. We love that idea, too, but we like this "little black dress" version of crème fraîche even better. For every ½ cup creamy, thick nonfat Greek yogurt, like Fage, whisk in 2 tablespoons honey until smooth. Then pop a dollop on your favorite desserts. Cover and keep refrigerated for up to 1 week.

Calories 200 • Total Fat 7g • Saturated Fat 4g • Carbohydrates 32.5g
Protein 4.5g • Dietary Fiber 2.5 g • Sodium 121mg

PROFESSOR POSITIVE
The Importance of Having Fun

Sometimes things are so busy it's hard to set aside any time for leisure. Interestingly, not only are leisure activities fun, they are also good for you. Research reported in the September 2009 issue of *Psychosomatic Medicine* has shown that individuals who spend more time on restorative activities (like spending time in nature, taking vacations, doing enjoyable activities with their friends, exercising, or even just spending time on a hobby) not only have greater life satisfaction and more happiness, they also have lower blood pressure, lower stress hormones, and sleep more soundly at night.

Strawberry Cheesecake Frozen Yogurt

Unlike homemade ice cream, which often requires a cooked custard base, this dairy treat whips up in minutes—no cooking involved, just an ice cream maker.

Makes about 6 cups; serves 6 • Prep Time: 5 minutes • Freezing Time: according to the ice cream maker directions

2   cups fresh **strawberries**, stemmed and coarsely chopped

1   cup sugar

8   ounces Neufchâtel or cream cheese, at room temperature

3   cups nonfat **Greek yogurt**, such as Fage

1   tablespoon fresh **lemon juice**

1   In a bowl, combine the strawberries and sugar. In a second bowl, beat the cheese and yogurt with an electric mixer until smooth. Beat in the lemon juice. With a rubber spatula, fold in the strawberry mixture until well mixed.

2   Transfer to an ice cream maker and process according to the manufacturer's directions.

Calories 311 • Total Fat 9g • Saturated Fat 5g • Carbohydrates 48.5g
Protein 11g • Dietary Fiber 1g • Sodium 221mg

What is laughter yoga?

A hearty laugh is a good workout for more than just the heart muscle. According to a study at the University of Maryland, in ScienceDaily.com on May 5, 2008, it also exercises the diaphragm, stomach, respiratory, facial, leg, and back muscles. Laughter is a great aerobic exercise because it increases the body's ability to use oxygen, sort of an internal jogging.

Laughter reduces stress levels, elevates mood, and improves emotional health. It releases endorphins into the body, which are the body's natural mood enhancers. Laughter also gives perspective on life, changes the way the mind thinks, and suppresses feelings of being overwhelmed.

The concept of Laughter Yoga is based on a scientific fact that the body cannot differentiate between fake and real laughter. One gets the same physiological and psychological benefits from both. Here's how it works:

Laughter is simulated as a full-body exercise in a group setting; with eye contact and childlike playfulness, it soon turns into real and contagious laughter. The concept was launched by Dr. Madan Kataria, a physician from India, who began the first Laughter Club in a park in 1995.

WOULD SOMEONE JUST TELL ME . . .

Q: Why did you use so many nutrient-dense foods in this book?

A: Nutrient density is the amount of nutritional value per calorie of a food.

You get the most "bang for your buck" (or karma for your calories!) when you eat food with a high level of nutrients, relative to the calories it contains. Think of all the nutrients in a handful of dried fruit, compared to the same amount of fruit snacks. They both contain about the same amount of calories. But the dried fruit has many more vitamins and minerals, while the fruit snacks are mostly sugar; so the dried fruit is considered more nutrient dense.

Classic Creamy Cheesecake with Fresh Berries

Sometimes this crustless Sara Lee®-style cheesecake is the only edible answer to any of life's pressing questions. Although classic in flavor, this trimmed-down version is a shocking example of how change is actually a welcome friend! The key is nonfat Greek yogurt, which has a texture like sour cream because it has been strained; other yogurts use thickeners instead. However, even Greek yogurt needs to be relieved of any accumulated liquid before you use it in baking. This treat is destined to become a perfect reason to give the gift of cheesecake to yourself or a friend . . . any day of the week.

Makes 1 (9-inch) cheesecake; serves 8 • Prep Time: 20 minutes • Cook Time: 25 minutes

8 ounces Neufchâtel or low-fat cream cheese, at room temperature

8 ounces nonfat **Greek yogurt**, such as Fage, drained of excess liquid

⅔ cup sugar

1 large **egg**

4 large **egg** whites, or ½ cup refrigerated egg white product

¼ cup all-purpose flour

½ teaspoon almond or vanilla extract

TOPPING

8 ounces nonfat **Greek yogurt**, such as Fage, drained of excess liquid

3 tablespoons sugar

1 teaspoon vanilla extract

2 cups fresh **blueberries**, **strawberries**, or **raspberries**

1. Preheat the oven to 350°F. Coat a deep 9-inch pie pan with a small amount of oil or butter.

2. To make the filling, combine the cheese, yogurt, and sugar in the bowl of a mixer or food processor and blend until light and creamy. Add the egg and egg whites, flour, and almond extract and mix or process until smooth. Pour the filling into the prepared pan.

3. Bake for 25 to 27 minutes, until the filling has just set. Leave the oven on and transfer the cheesecake to a wire rack to cool slightly for 10 minutes.

4. For the topping, whisk together the yogurt, sugar, and vanilla in a medium bowl until smooth. Spoon the topping over the cheesecake and smooth with a spatula. Return to the oven to bake for 8 to 10 minutes longer, until the topping has set. Remove from the oven and let cool completely before serving. Serve with fresh berries.

Calories 178 • Total Fat 7g • Saturated Fat 4g • Carbohydrates 21g
Protein 7g • Dietary Fiber 0g • Sodium 152 mg

My hair was long enough for my stylist to color, highlight, and style!

~Roz Varon, television anchor/reporter

Celebration Chocolate Cake

We believe it's not a cookbook without a chocolate cake. And this one-bowl, dark chocolate little number is an especially perfect match for our devotion to pumpkin and cocoa. Adapted from a recipe by dessert chef Emily Luchetti, our version ditched some of the fat and sugar but kept the joyful flavor. Use a large bowl, so you can easily whisk the batter together. Let the chocolate glaze cool a bit, and it will thicken like ganache.

Serves 14 • Prep Time: 15 minutes • Cook Time: 35 minutes

CAKE

1 cup **buttermilk**

1 cup water

⅓ cup vegetable oil

⅓ cup unsweetened **applesauce**

1½ cups sugar

2 large **eggs**

1 teaspoon baking soda

Pinch of salt

2 cups all-purpose flour

¾ cup unsweetened **cocoa** powder

FILLING

8 ounces Neufchâtel or low-fat cream cheese, at room temperature

⅓ cup canned **pumpkin** puree (not seasoned pie filling)

¼ cup **honey, agave nectar**, or **sorghum**

½ teaspoon ground **cinnamon**

¼ teaspoon freshly grated **nutmeg**

GLAZE

½ cup half-and-half

¾ cup semisweet **chocolate** chips

TOPPING

Seedless **red grapes**, whole **blackberries**, pistachios, and curls of fresh **orange peel**

1 Preheat the oven to 350°F. Coat 2 (9-inch) round cake pans with a small amount of oil or butter; dust with flour and tap out any excess over the sink. Set aside.

2 For the cake, whisk the buttermilk, water, oil, applesauce, sugar, eggs, baking soda, and salt together in a very large bowl until well blended. Whisk in the flour and cocoa powder until smooth. Divide the batter between the prepared pans.

3 Bake for 32 to 35 minutes, until the top springs back when lightly touched. Let cool in the pans for 10 minutes, then invert onto wire racks to cool.

4 For the filling, whisk the cheese, pumpkin, sweetener, cinnamon, and nutmeg in a medium bowl until well blended. Place one cake layer on a plate. Spread with the filling, and top with the second layer.

5 For the glaze, heat the half-and-half in a saucepan over medium-high heat until it starts to bubble. Remove from the heat and add the chocolate chips. Let sit for 1 minute, then whisk until glossy, smooth, and dark. Let cool for 20 minutes, or until slightly thickened. Pour half of the glaze over the cake; pour the remaining glaze into a small bowl to pass at the table. Gently heat the glaze over simmering water, or on the defrost setting of the microwave, so it's pourable right before serving. Casually arrange the topping ingredients on top of the glazed cake.

TIP: If you don't have buttermilk, substitute 2 teaspoons fresh lemon juice or vinegar in 1 cup milk. Stir and let sit for 5 minutes before using.

Calories 336 • Total Fat 14g • Saturated Fat 6g
Carbohydrates 51g • Protein 6g • Dietary Fiber 3g
Sodium 88mg

WHO KNEW?

Q. Does cinnamon contain any health benefits?

A. According to the National Center for Biotechnology Information report July 24, 2010, "Studying the active components of cinnamon extract could lead to development of potent anti-tumor agents or complementary and alternative medicine for the treatment of diverse cancers." Due to cinnamon's high antioxidant and anti-inflammatory properties, Bharat Aggarwal, PhD, professor in MD Anderson Cancer Center's Department of Experimental Therapeutics sees the incorporation of cinnamon into one's diet as positive.

Joy is a state of mind, and celebration is the outward manifestation of joy . . . the human way of sharing inner personal joy.

~Lon Lane, president, International Caterers Association Educational Foundation, and co-owner, Inspired Occasions

Baked Lemon-Spice Apples

Put this dessert in the oven an hour or so before serving. Your family and friends will be greeted by both the aroma and the anticipation of the edible therapy of this dish. Also delicious for any time of day, these baked apples make fruit a treat that is fit for your own or your company's delight.

Serves 4 • Prep Time: 15 minutes • Cook Time: 55 to 60 minutes

4   tart **apples**, such as Granny Smith, peeled, cored, and sliced

½   teaspoon ground **cinnamon**

½   teaspoon ground **nutmeg**

½   cup dried **cherries**

2   tablespoons all-purpose flour

¼   cup **honey**, **agave nectar**, or **sorghum**

½   teaspoon grated **lemon** zest

½   cup **apple juice** or **apple cider**, heated

2   tablespoons chopped **walnuts**

1   Preheat the oven to 350°F. Coat a 9-inch square baking pan with a small amount of oil or butter. Add the apples, cinnamon, nutmeg, cherries, and flour to the prepared pan and toss until the apples are well coated with the spice mixture. In a small bowl, mix the sweetener, lemon zest, and hot apple juice until well blended. Pour over the apple mixture.

2   Cover the pan tightly with aluminum foil and bake for 45 minutes. Uncover, sprinkle with the walnuts, and bake for 10 to 15 minutes longer, until bubbly.

Calories 265 • Total Fat 3g • Saturated Fat 0g • Carbohydrates 62g
Protein 2g • Dietary Fiber 3.5g • Sodium 5mg

Gingersnap-Crusted Pumpkin Pie

Who needs a lot of crust when the delicious, creamy, spicy filling is so good? Plus, this crumb crust is much easier to make than pastry! Grate from a whole nutmeg for the best flavor, but ground nutmeg spices it up just fine.

Serves 8 • Prep Time: 15 minutes • Cook Time: 55 to 65 minutes

GINGERSNAP CRUST

½ cup gingersnap crumbs (from about 12 thin packaged gingersnap cookies, such as Anna's)

PUMPKIN FILLING

½ cup **honey**, **agave nectar**, or **sorghum**

1 teaspoon ground **cinnamon**

½ teaspoon freshly grated **nutmeg**

½ teaspoon ground **ginger**

2 large **egg** yolks, beaten

1 (15-ounce) can **pumpkin** puree (not seasoned pie filling)

1 (12-ounce) can evaporated (not condensed) **milk**

2 large **egg** whites

1 Preheat the oven to 425°F. Coat a 9-inch pie pan with a small amount of oil or butter.

2 For the crust, sprinkle the gingersnap crumbs on the bottom and up the sides of the pie pan and gently press to set.

3 For the filling, combine the sweetener, cinnamon, nutmeg, ginger, egg yolks, pumpkin, and evaporated milk in a medium bowl and stir with a mixing spoon until well blended. In a second medium bowl, beat the egg whites until stiff peaks form. With a spatula, fold the egg whites into the pumpkin mixture until you can't see the whites anymore. Spoon the filling into the prepared pan.

4 Bake for 15 minutes, then reduce the heat to 350°F and bake for 40 to 50 minutes longer, until a knife inserted near the center comes out clean. Cool on a wire rack.

Calories 130 • Total Fat 4g • Saturated Fat 1.5g • Carbohydrates 20g
Protein 4.5g • Dietary Fiber 3.5g • Sodium 106mg

Carrot Cake Cupcakes with Pineapple–Cream Cheese Frosting

Who doesn't love carrot cake—or cupcakes? These luscious beauties, trimmed down with egg whites, applesauce, and low-fat cream cheese for the frosting, encourage you to savor your favorite treat in a handy travel size!

Makes 16 cupcakes; serves 16 • Prep Time: 25 minutes • Cook Time: 20 minutes

CUPCAKES

1⅓ cups old-fashioned rolled **oats**

1 cup all-purpose flour

2 teaspoons baking powder

¼ teaspoon baking soda

½ teaspoon ground **cinnamon**

¼ teaspoon salt

¾ cup unsweetened **applesauce**

½ cup skim **milk**

⅓ cup wildflower or clover **honey**

¼ cup refrigerated **egg** white product or egg whites

1 tablespoon **grapeseed oil** or **canola oil**

1½ cups finely shredded **carrots**

½ cup golden **raisins**

PINEAPPLE–CREAM CHEESE FROSTING

8 ounces Neufchâtel or low-fat cream cheese, at room temperature

1 (8-ounce) can crushed **pineapple**, with juice

½ cup confectioners' sugar, or more as necessary

1 Preheat the oven to 400°F. Line 16 muffins cups with paper liners and set aside.

2 For the cupcakes, place the rolled oats in a food processor or blender and process until the mixture resembles coarse flour. Transfer the oat flour to a medium bowl and stir in the all-purpose flour, baking powder, baking soda, cinnamon, and salt. In a second medium bowl, stir the applesauce, milk, honey, egg white product, and oil together until well blended. Stir the applesauce mixture into the oat flour mixture until just moistened. Stir in the carrots and raisins. Spoon the batter into the prepared muffin cups, filling two-thirds full.

3 Bake for 18 to 20 minutes, until a toothpick inserted into the center comes out clean. Let cool on a wire rack for 5 minutes.

4 For the frosting, place the cheese and pineapple in a bowl and mix with a hand mixer until fluffy. Beat in the confectioners' sugar until the frosting has a spreadable consistency. Frost the cupcakes.

Calories 160 • Total Fat 4.5g
Saturated Fat 2g • Carbohydrates 26.5g
Protein 4g • Dietary Fiber 1.5g
Sodium 102mg

TREAT OF THE DAY

The American Film Institute's Top 10 Inspiring Movies

In 2006, the American Film Institute (AFI) jury of fifteen hundred film artists, critics, and historians selected their list of the most inspiring movies of all time. Here is their Top 10:

It's a Wonderful Life

To Kill a Mockingbird

Schindler's List

Rocky

Mr. Smith Goes to Washington

E.T.—The Extra-Terrestrial

The Grapes of Wrath

Breaking Away

Miracle on 34th Street

Saving Private Ryan

The secret of getting
ahead is getting started.

~Mark Twain

CHAPTER TWO

Breakfast

Brand New Day

"Accommodating to change is a recipe for happiness,"

~according to our friend, Shawsie Branton

We agree, and have inserted some ways to start your day with nontraditional

goodies. As you are enjoying these new twists on old favorites (think broiled

grapefruit or flax in your flapjacks), carry that thinking with you all day.

This chapter focuses on the moments at the beginning of the day that give us

pleasure, such as a morning latte, food that we can feel good about eating or

drinking because they are a wealth of nurturing for the mind, body, and spirit.

So grab your imagination as you redefine each day for change . . . try a

frittata instead of a scrambled egg, for example. Shaking things up, in a small

way, can feel like a big vacation from your routine.

Another cup of coffee . . . please!

The evidence is out: Coffee contains large amounts of antioxidants that improve health. Other research has suggested coffee can help prevent cognitive decline and can boost vision and heart health.

According to findings reported in March 2011 in *Stroke: Journal of the American Heart Association*, women in the study who drank more than 1 cup of coffee a day had a 22 percent to 25 percent lower risk of stroke than those who drank less. Stroke is the third leading cause of death in the United States, behind heart disease and cancer.

"We used to worry that [coffee] raises blood pressure and causes increased heart rate, but it appears to be less risky than we thought," says physician Claudette Brooks, spokeswoman for the American Stroke Association.

Top of the Week Latte

Why not toast the new day with a healthy breakfast libation? Cuddle up with a spiced blueberry applesauce muffin (page 49), the morning news (in your favorite format), and enjoy!

Serves 4 or 1, if you like refills • Prep Time: 5 minutes
Cook Time: 5 minutes

2   cups nonfat **almond milk** or rice milk

1⅓ cups hot freshly brewed dark roast espresso **coffee**

4   **cinnamon** sticks

1   Heat the milk in a saucepan set over medium-low heat. Whisk briskly to create foam. Pour the coffee into 4 cups. Pour in the milk, holding back the foam with a spoon. Spoon the foam over the top. Swizzle each latte with a cinnamon stick to add a boost of flavor to your cup of antioxidants. Beautiful!

Calories 48 • Total Fat 0g • Saturated Fat 0g
Carbohydrates 7g • Protein 4g • Dietary Fiber 1g
Sodium 62mg

I didn't have to sleep more than eight hours a night to feel rested, almost one year after treatment ended.

~Margaret Reynolds, managing principal, Reynolds Consulting, LLC

Almond Milk Orange Caesar

A blended drink called Orange Caesar was invented in the 1920s, but the "smoothie" craze didn't begin until the invention of the Waring Blender in 1939, when people started to create recipes for fruit and vegetable drinks by that name. Now our own version rules, so we call it an Orange Caesar. We make it with almond milk and add whey protein concentrate for a drink that tastes just as good but with a bit more power.

Makes 1 drink • Prep Time: 5 minutes

½ cup vanilla-flavored **almond milk**, rice milk, or skim milk

½ cup **orange juice**

½ teaspoon vanilla or **orange** extract

1 tablespoon whey protein concentrate, such as Bob's Red Mill (optional)

½ cup ice cubes

1 Combine the milk, orange juice, vanilla, whey, and ice cubes in a blender and blend until smooth.

Calories 125 • Total Fat 0.5g • Saturated Fat 0g • Carbohydrates 21g
Protein 8g • Dietary Fiber 0.3g • Sodium 107mg

WOULD SOMEONE JUST TELL ME . . .

Q: How do I get out of the habit of labeling myself as being a "bad" person for eating a certain food or a "good" person for eating another food?

A: We cannot emphasize this enough and would stand at the top of a mountain and shout it if we could: Food is *not* a moral issue. You are not "good" for eating only celery today, nor are you "bad" for eating a half-gallon of mint chip ice cream. There is no such thing as the food police.

Soothe Thee Fruit Smoothie

Why would a person want to drink her fruit? Because a smoothie has such "a-peel"! Change the fruit and change the flavor to blueberry banana, strawberry banana, or banana orange.

Serves 1 • Prep Time: 5 minutes

1 cup frozen unsweetened **strawberries** or **blueberries**, thawed, or ½ **banana**

½ cup nonfat **Greek yogurt**, such as Fage

1 cup **orange juice**

1 cup water, or ice

1 Combine the fruit, yogurt, orange juice, and water or ice in a blender and process until creamy. Pour into a cup and serve.

TIP: When your banana ripens a little too much—and there's always at least one that gets too ripe to eat as is—freeze it unpeeled. Then peel it frozen, carefully chunk, and use in this smoothie. Or dip it frozen in chocolate syrup for a sweet indulgence.

Calories 125 • Total Fat 0.5g • Saturated Fat 0g • Carbohydrates 21g
Protein 8g • Dietary Fiber 3g • Sodium 107mg

WHO KNEW?

Q: Why use Greek yogurt instead of another kind of yogurt?

A: Greek yogurt can have twice as much protein as regular yogurt, leaving you feeling full and satisfied. It can also have less sodium by up to 50 percent than regular yogurt. If you want to lower your carbohydrate count, as well, regular yogurts have 15 to 17 grams of carbohydrates per cup, whereas Greek yogurt averages around 9 grams.

People who believe in luck collect daily events as evidence that they either have it or not.

By Jerry Wyckoff, PhD

You can collect daily events as evidence of good or bad days. Bad days are characterized by the little things that happened which get labeled negatively, such as the knee we bumped getting out of the car or the frustrating experience of misplacing our car keys and needing to get a ride to work. One or more of these things happen and suddenly, you're having a "bad day." You know the drill.

But you can collect the so-called good things from the day, just as easily as the bad, by noting the big smile your coworker gave you this morning, the kiss from your child whom you left at school, the warm feeling you had when you heard that song you like, or the knowledge that you are holding a cookbook that gives you easy appetizers to begin a meal in a happy frame of mind.

Days, like everything, are actually neutral, neither good nor bad. It's all in how you look at things, not in the things themselves. So spend your days looking for good things and putting what you consider to be bad things in perspective.

On the other hand, in the book *The Human Side of Cancer*, Jimmie C. Holland, MD, addresses a situation in which holding onto a healthy perspective on being a cancer survivor may be difficult: "Trying to put on a 'happy face' to pretend you are feeling confident, when in fact you are feeling tremendously fearful and upset, can have a downside. By feigning confidence and ease about your illness and its treatment, you may cut off help and support from others. The tyranny of positive thinking can inhibit you from getting the help you may need out of fear of disappointing your loved ones or admitting to a personality some people think is fatal."

Attitude, personality, and emotion all play a part in how you see the world. So if you are having difficulty getting back in the swing of life because you are anxious or worried or fearful, know that feeling this way from time to time is normal. If every day is filled with depression, however, and you are unable to collect any "good things" from day to day and reframe your situation, consult with a psychologist, social worker, or a good friend who will listen and support you. You'll feel better and look better, and you may find that you become healthier. Good days, like good meals, don't just happen; you make them happen by how you think about them.

Apple Cider Oatmeal with Fresh Apple Dippers

In just 30 minutes (or overnight in a slow cooker), you can have a delicious breakfast that starts your day off right—and keeps you satisfied, longer. Using steel-cut (Irish) oats—chopped whole oat kernels—gives you the benefits of whole grains, while cooking them in apple juice adds flavor. Fresh slices of apple as dippers help you scoop up every caramel-like bite. Be sure to leave them unpeeled because you want the nutrients under the skin. Look for steel-cut oats in the specialty flour or organic ingredients aisle, if not with all the other oatmeal products. For a slow-cooker version, combine the cider, oats, dried cherries, and salt in a slow cooker. Cover and cook on the low setting overnight.

Serves 2 • Prep Time: 5 minutes • Cook Time: 20 minutes

1½ cups **apple juice** or **apple cider**

½ cup steel-cut (Irish) **oats**

2 tablespoons sweetened dried **cherries** or **blueberries**

¼ teaspoon salt

1 tart **apple**, cored and cut into 8 pieces (unpeeled, because you want the nutrients under the skin)

1 Bring the apple juice to a boil in a medium saucepan over medium-high heat. Stir in the oats, cherries, and salt. Reduce the heat and simmer, stirring occasionally, for about 17 minutes, until the oats are al dente, or for about 20 minutes, until softened. Spoon into bowls and serve with apple dippers.

Calories 235 • Total Fat 55g • Saturated Fat 0g • Carbohydrates 54.5g
Protein 3g • Dietary Fiber 3.5g • Sodium 379mg

STEEL-CUT (IRISH) OATS

ROLLED OATS

WHO KNEW?

Q: What is the difference between oats?

A: Three types of oats all start from the same grains, but they are cut differently:

Rolled oats are whole oats rolled flat and steamed slightly to make them cook faster.

Quick oats are rolled oats that have been ground up a little bit more so they cook even faster than rolled oats.

Steel-cut (Irish) oats, the whole raw oat cut into small chunks, have a nutty flavor that rolled oats lack and are definitely chewier.

If there is one area where steel-cut oats have a health edge, it's in their lack of processing. Because the rolled oats are steamed, there's a chance steel-cut oats contain more vitamins and minerals. Since both kinds are usually eaten cooked, however, whatever advantage steel-cut oats have is lost, unless you eat them raw.

DID YOU HEAR THE NEWS?

Heart health . . . it's in the oats!

According to a May 7, 2010, Mayo Clinic staff report, *Cholesterol: Top 5 Foods to Lower Your Numbers*, "Oatmeal contains soluble fiber, which reduces low-density lipoprotein (LDL), the 'bad' cholesterol, by reducing the absorption of cholesterol into your bloodstream. Eating 5 to 10 grams or more of soluble fiber a day decreases your total LDL cholesterol, and 1½ cups of cooked oatmeal provide 6 grams of fiber. If you add fruit, such as a banana, you'll add about 4 more grams of fiber."

QUICK OATS

Spiced Blueberry Applesauce Muffins

Some of our favorite flavors come together to celebrate taste, texture, and great health. Make a batch, individually wrap the muffins well, and freeze for up to 3 months. You may prefer golden flaxseed because it doesn't have the "horse food" flavor, some say, and the color is better in the final product.

Makes 12 to 15 muffins • Prep Time: 10 minutes • Cook Time: 16 to 18 minutes

1¼ cups whole wheat flour

1¼ cups old-fashioned rolled **oats**

1 teaspoon baking powder

½ teaspoon baking soda

¼ teaspoon salt

1 teaspoon ground **cinnamon**

1 tablespoon milled **flaxseed**

1 cup unsweetened **applesauce**

½ cup **buttermilk**

½ cup firmly packed **brown sugar**

2 tablespoons **grapeseed oil** or **canola oil**

1 large **egg**, beaten

¾ cup fresh or thawed frozen **blueberries**

1 Preheat the oven to 375°F. Line 12 muffin cups with paper liners.

2 In a large bowl combine the flour, oats, baking powder, baking soda, salt, cinnamon, and flaxseed. In a medium bowl, combine the applesauce, buttermilk, brown sugar, oil, and egg. Stir the applesauce mixture into the flour mixture until just moist. Fold in the blueberries. Fill the muffin cups equally, about two-thirds full.

3 Bake for 16 to 18 minutes, until a toothpick inserted in the center of a muffin comes out clean.

Calories 144 • Total Fat 3.5g • Saturated Fat 0.5g
Carbohydrates 26g • Protein 3.5g • Dietary Fiber 3g • Sodium 94mg

I got to that place where I felt like my body, mind, and spirit were my own again.

~Elaine Nelson, elementary school teacher

Wendy's Wonderful Granola

From our friend and Kansas beekeeper, Wendy Webb, comes a great old-fashioned recipe (made with honey, of course!). As a gift from your kitchen, this granola is a star. It can be used to make a breakfast parfait, layered with yogurt and fresh fruit; eaten alone as a snack; or spooned over baked fruit for an easy fruit crisp.

Makes 4 cups; serves 8 • Prep Time: 10 minutes • Cook Time: 20 to 30 minutes

2 cups old-fashioned rolled or steel-cut (Irish) **oats**

1 teaspoon baking powder

1 large **egg**, beaten

1½ cups vanilla-flavored **almond milk**, rice milk, or skim milk

½ cup **honey**

½ cup coarsely chopped **walnuts**

½ cup sweetened dried **cranberries** or raisins

1 **apple**, peeled, cored, and finely chopped, or ½ cup **applesauce**

1 Preheat the oven to 350°F. Line a large rimmed baking sheet or an 8 or 9-inch casserole dish with aluminum foil. Coat the foil with a thin layer of butter or oil.

2 Combine the oats and baking powder in a large bowl. In a small bowl, whisk the egg, milk, and honey together. Pour over the oat mixture and toss to blend. Fold in the walnuts, cranberries, and apple. Spread the mixture into the prepared pan.

3 Bake for 20 to 30 minutes, until the edges are slightly brown and the granola is crisp. Store in an airtight container for up to 2 weeks.

Calories 62 • Total Fat 13.5g • Saturated Fat 2g • Carbohydrates 88g Protein 13g • Dietary Fiber 6g • Sodium 219mg

Bellini-Style Peaches with Raspberries

Here's an easy way to dress up fruit without fussing over it. If peaches aren't in season, but you still hanker for this dish, use frozen unsweetened sliced peaches thawed and drizzled with a little honey to sweeten.

Serves 4 • Prep Time: 5 minutes

4   ripe **peaches**, pitted, peeled, and sliced

1   cup fresh **raspberries**

    Honey

2   cups sparkling **cider**, **grape juice**, or **pomegranate juice**, chilled

1   Divide the peaches and the raspberries among 4 glass bowls or parfait glasses. Drizzle with honey to taste, and fill the rest of the glass with sparkling cider. Serve with a spoon.

Calories 172 • Total Fat 0.5g • Saturated Fat 0g
Carbohydrates 21g • Protein 2g • Dietary Fiber 4g
Sodium 6mg

DID YOU HEAR THE NEWS?

Alcohol? Not so much.

Published in the August 30, 2010, *Journal of Clinical Oncology*, the Life After Cancer Epidemiology Study (LACE) reported that breast cancer survivors who consume more than three alcoholic drinks per week were more likely to have a recurrence of their tumor. Postmenopausal risk increased by 40 percent, and the combined group risk for pre- and postmenopausal women was 34 percent.

When comparing survivors who drink more than three alcoholic drinks per week to survivors who abstain or drink far less alcohol on a weekly basis, the difference in tumor recurrence was significant. Prior research has demonstrated that alcohol consumption may influence the risk of developing an initial breast cancer, but this is the first evidence linking alcohol consumption with breast cancer recurrence.

Retro Broiled Pink Grapefruit

This retro breakfast dish deserves a comeback, so here it is with a new twist—honey, agave nectar, or sorghum instead of sugar, to add just a little sweetness. Enjoy this with an egg scrambled with your favorite vegetables.

Serves 4 • Prep Time: 5 minutes • Cook Time: 3 to 5 minutes

2   pink **grapefruit**

¼   cup **honey**, **agave nectar**, or **sorghum**

1   Preheat the broiler. Cut each grapefruit in half crosswise. Use a sharp knife to cut each section to loosen the flesh from the membrane and remove any seeds. Drizzle each grapefruit half with 1 tablespoon sweetener. Arrange the grapefruit in the broiler pan, cut side up.

2   Broil for 3 to 5 minutes, until lightly browned on top. Serve warm.

Calories 73 • Total Fat 0.2g • Saturated Fat 0g • Carbohydrates 18g
Protein 1g • Dietary Fiber 3.5g • Sodium 2mg

WHO KNEW?

Q: I like to drink grapefruit juice but hear that it can interfere with some of my prescription medications. Is that true?

A: Yes. In a Mayo Clinic online newsletter report by Katherine Zeratsky, RD, LD, November 3, 2011, she noted that grapefruit juice, other grapefruit products, and certain other citrus fruits can interfere with several kinds of prescription medications. "Don't take these interactions lightly, as some can cause potentially dangerous health problems," Zeratsky said. "Certain chemicals that grapefruit products and citrus fruits contain can interfere with the enzymes that break down (metabolize) various medications in your digestive system. Check with your doctor or pharmacist before consuming any grapefruit products or citrus fruits if you take prescription medications. Simply taking your medication and grapefruit product at different times may not stop the interaction."

Look at cancer on the flip side. I see it as an opportunity to be proactive and make lifestyle changes. I see it as a fresh and new beginning.

~Lori C. Lober, business owner and author

Blackberry-Lavender Compote

This warm blackberry dish is an example of how just a little dried lavender makes blackberries taste berry-er in a perfect treat for breakfast, brunch, or even a vitamin-packed snack. The compote is also delicious with a dollop of unsweetened plain yogurt and granola, or for dessert over frozen yogurt. Look for lavender buds in health food or spice retailers specializing in edible herbs, such as Penzeys and Dean & Deluca.

Serves 4 • Prep Time: 5 minutes • Cook Time: 5 minutes

4 cups fresh or frozen, thawed, **blackberries**

¾ teaspoon organic dried **lavender** buds

½ cup **honey, agave nectar**, or **sorghum**

1 tablespoon fresh **lemon juice**

1 Combine the blackberries, lavender, and sweetener in a saucepan over medium-high heat. Bring to a boil. Cook, stirring, for 5 minutes, or until the blackberries are soft and juicy. Remove from the heat. Add the lemon juice. Serve warm or cold.

Calories 101 • Total Fat 0.8g • Saturated Fat 0g • Carbohydrates 23g
Protein 2g • Dietary Fiber 10.5g • Sodium 5mg

According to the July 2010 *Medicine and Science in Sports and Exercise*, the 2010 American College of Sports Medicine (ACSM) Roundtable on Exercise Guidelines for Cancer Survivors revealed that clinicians have historically advised cancer patients to rest and avoid activity; however, current science shows this one-size-fits-all guidance is outdated.

The lead author of the cancer recommendations and a presenter at the ACSM Annual Meeting, Kathryn Schmitz, PhD, MPH, FACSM, says: "We're seeing better everyday function and overall higher quality of life for cancer survivors who exercise. In preliminary observations, breast cancer survivors experienced improved body image as a result of a regular physical activity program. Add that to improved aerobic fitness and strength, decreased fatigue, and increased quality of life, and exercise proves to be a crucial part of recovery for cancer survivors."

The report did advise using "specific programming adaptations based on treatment-related adverse effects." Check with your health care practitioner to ensure safe and effective exercise routines.

WOULD SOMEONE JUST TELL ME . . .

Q: How do I talk with my provider about my concerns over what I should or should not be eating?

A: This is often not a subject in which providers are well versed. Many have limited training in nutritional science, so referrals to specialists, such as dietitians and therapists, might be necessary. It is important to express that you need and want personalized information on this topic, so you can choose the foods that will take into account your nutritional needs, as well as your taste buds. Taking control over getting your own unique needs met will be empowering; it is important to form a collaborative and integrative team to do so. Ask that your nutrition expert work closely with your medical providers, so that both are on the same page with you.

Lox of Love: Smoked Salmon with Bagels and Green Onion Cream Cheese

One of the most popular breakfast items in the world packs a high-protein (and salt) punch, but it's a wonderful celebration breakfast every once in a while. Low-fat cream cheese, full of cool, fresh taste and texture, partners perfectly with the thin-sliced salmon. Make your own fancy cream cheese spread, and you've got your own deli anytime you're in the mood.

Serves 4 • Prep Time: 10 minutes

12 ounces very thinly sliced smoked **salmon**

4 whole grain bagels, thinly sliced

GREEN ONION CREAM CHEESE

8 ounces Neufchâtel or low-fat cream cheese, at room temperature

2 tablespoons skim **milk**

¼ cup chopped **green onion**

½ teaspoon ground black pepper

Fresh **lemon** wedges, for garnish

1 Set out the salmon and bagels. For the spread, place the cheese, skim milk, green onion, and pepper in a blender or food processor and blend until the green onion is very finely chopped. Transfer to a bowl with your favorite spreader. To serve, slather a thin layer of the cream cheese on a slice of bagel and top with smoked salmon. Add a squeeze of lemon, if you like.

Calories 517 • Total Fat 18g • Saturated Fat 8g • Carbohydrates 56g Protein 32g • Dietary Fiber 2g • Sodium 1330mg

ON THE UPSWING

Serenity and mindfulness, with a focus on being grateful for what we have, allow us to forget about our worries . . . sort of a "joy ride" on a warm summer day.

~Donna Pelletier, cancer survivorship advocate

WHO KNEW?

Q: What is lox? And is it good for me?

A: The type of smoked salmon called lox goes through immersion in brine followed by rapid smoking over high heat or slowly smoking over a low temperature. The good news is that it is high in omega-3 fatty acids, a healthy type of fat. Omega-3 fatty acids are a necessity for proper brain functioning and help maintain heart health by lowering triglycerides, slightly lowering blood pressure, reducing the risk of heart arrhythmia, and slowing the growth of arterial plaque.

Smoked salmon, however, contains less omega-3 fat than fresh salmon. The smoking process increases the salt content of salmon, which may be of concern to individuals monitoring their salt intake. A 3-ounce single serving of smoked salmon has 784 grams of sodium, while a serving of lox contains about 2,000 grams of sodium. According to federal dietary guidelines, most individuals should consume no more than 2,300 milligrams of sodium per day, and people at high risk for hypertension should aim for less than 1,500 milligrams a day. So one slice should do your taste buds and heart a favor, if you're watching your salt intake. If you can find wild-caught smoked salmon, it's better for you and the environment.

Potato Frittata Twist

This is so good, you won't believe it's this easy! In Spain and Portugal, this favorite comforting dish of sliced potatoes, thinly sliced peppers, garlic, and olive oil cooked in an egg batter is sliced and served in wedges, hot or cold. It's so quick to make, it's perfect for a soothing "I'm hungry right now" dinner. Of course, a frittata is also great for breakfast. This recipe calls for baked potatoes, so plan on preparing them the night before. If you don't have baked potatoes on hand, prick the potatoes all over with a paring knife and microwave on high for 7 to 8 minutes, until tender. Then slice. The good-for-you foods also include fresh lemon juice, garlic, and olive oil in the Work of Art Drizzle.

Serves 4 • Prep Time: 15 minutes • Cook Time: 8 minutes plus 1 hour if baking the potatoes

1½ tablespoons Work of Art Drizzle (page 145), divided

3 medium cold baked russet potatoes, thinly sliced

1 cup very thinly sliced jarred **roasted red peppers**

¼ cup chopped fresh Italian **parsley**

2 large **eggs**

2 large **egg** whites

Salt and pepper

1 Place a large skillet over medium-high heat and brush the bottom with about 2 teaspoons of the Work of Art Drizzle. Arrange the potatoes, then the peppers in the skillet. Cook for 5 minutes, without stirring, until the potatoes are warm. Drizzle on the remaining Work of Art Drizzle and sprinkle with the parsley. In a bowl, whisk the eggs and egg whites with salt and pepper and pour over the vegetables. Cook, covered, without stirring, for about 8 minutes, until the egg mixture is solid when you shake the pan. Remove from the heat, slice, and serve.

Calories 173 • Total Fat 2.5g • Saturated Fat 1g • Carbohydrates 30g
Protein 8g • Dietary Fiber 3.6g • Sodium 66mg

Banana Flax-Jacks
with Blackberry-Lavender Compote

These pancakes will become your new favorite for all the right reasons. They are so simple to make because they start with a mix you've made ahead of time, with added flax and yogurt for a boost of protein that keeps you rocking and rolling. These are also delicious with maple syrup, but Blackberry-Lavender Compote adds a new twist, with blackberry, lemon, and lavender super foods.

Makes 10 to 12 (4-inch) pancakes; serves 4 • Prep Time: 10 minutes • Cook Time: 20 minutes

HOMEMADE PANCAKE AND WAFFLE MIX

6 cups all-purpose flour

1½ teaspoons baking soda

1 tablespoon baking powder

1 tablespoon salt

3 tablespoons sugar

BANANA FLAX-JACKS

1 large **egg**, beaten

1 tablespoon **grapeseed oil** or **canola oil**

1 tablespoon **honey**

¼ cup nonfat **Greek yogurt**, such as Fage

¾ cup **almond milk**, rice milk, or skim milk

1 ripe **banana**, mashed

1 cup pancake and waffle mix

¼ cup golden milled **flaxseed**

¼ teaspoon salt

2 cups **Blackberry-Lavender** Compote (page 54)

1 For the mix, combine the flour, baking soda, baking powder, salt, and sugar. You should have about 6½ cups. The mix will keep for several months stored in an airtight container.

2 In a small bowl, whisk together the egg, oil, honey, yogurt, milk, and banana. Whisk in the pancake mix, milled flaxseed, and salt until smooth.

3 Heat a nonstick skillet over medium heat. Using a ¼ cup measure, pour the batter into the hot skillet. Cook until small bubbles start to appear on the surface, then flip and cook for 1 minute longer. Keep the pancakes warm in a covered dish as you make them. Serve warm with the compote.

Calories 109 • Total Fat 5g • Saturated Fat 1g • Carbohydrates 14g
Protein 4g • Dietary Fiber 1g • Sodium 229mg

PROFESSOR POSITIVE
Be grateful for what you have.

Sometimes it's hard to remember all of the good things going for us, especially when times are hard. When this happens to you, take a note from author Robert Emmons in his book *Thanks! How Practicing Gratitude Can Make You Happier*. Every night before you go to bed, write about three things that you are grateful for. These can be the "big things" like your family or "small things" like your favorite new song. Research has shown that doing this allows individuals to sleep better, experience less pain, and have more positive feelings. Give it a try tonight.

Sex. You knew we'd get around to it sooner or later.

"Sexual problems are among the most common and least talked about side effects of breast cancer treatment," according to researcher Susan R. Davis, MD, PhD, Monash University Medical School, in Monash, Australia, published in *The Journal of Sexual Medicine* in January 2011, "About 70% of the women in our study were experiencing a meaningful loss of desire and sexual function a full two years after diagnosis."

Use of aromatase inhibitors almost always results in extreme vaginal dryness related to estrogen depletion. As a result, sex can be extremely painful.

"Every woman who is put on these drugs should be told it is highly likely they will experience symptoms related to menopause, including vaginal dryness, but that isn't always happening," Davis says. "And women may be reluctant to talk about the issue with their oncologist."

Talk to your oncologist or nurse about recommending the appropriate treatment if you are experiencing any of these side effects to help you get your sex life back in the swing, too.

Fall Harvest Waffles with Maple Syrup

Create the cozy feeling of autumn in your kitchen any time of the year, any day of the week. Real maple syrup can vary in flavor according to the terrain and climate, much like wines made from grapes grown in different areas. Look for Grade B, a slightly darker and more flavorful maple syrup, to drizzle over these waffles full of the goodness of pumpkin.

Makes about 6 large waffles or 12 pancakes; serves 6 • Prep Time: 10 minutes • Cook Time: 15 minutes

2   cups Homemade Pancake and Waffle Mix (page 60)

½   cup packed **brown sugar**

½   teaspoon ground **cinnamon**

⅛   teaspoon ground **ginger**

1   tablespoon **grapeseed oil** or **canola oil**

1¼ cups **almond milk**, rice milk, or skim milk

⅓   cup **honey, agave nectar**, or **sorghum**

½   cup canned **pumpkin** puree (not seasoned pie filling)

1   large **egg**, beaten

    Maple syrup, for drizzling

1 In a medium bowl, combine the waffle mix, brown sugar, cinnamon, and ginger. Add the oil, milk, honey, pumpkin, and egg. Whisk until smooth.

2 For best results, bake in a waffle iron for about 90 seconds, according to the manufacturer's directions. Baking time will vary with the consistency of the batter and your preference for browning. Serve drizzled with maple syrup.

Calories 183 • Total Fat 2g • Saturated Fat 0.3g • Carbohydrates 40g Protein 2.5g • Dietary Fiber 2g • Sodium 162mg

We're stuck on maple syrup!

University of Rhode Island (URI) researcher Navindra Seeram, who specializes in medicinal plant research, has found more than twenty compounds in maple syrup from Canada that have been linked to human health.

The URI associate professor of biomedical and pharmaceutical sciences in URI's College of Pharmacy presented his findings at the March 21, 2010 American Chemical Society's annual meeting in San Francisco. He reported that several of these antioxidant compounds newly identified in maple syrup are also reported to have anticancer, antibacterial, and antidiabetic properties.

"We know that plants must have strong antioxidant mechanisms because they are in the sun throughout their lives," Seeram says. "We already know that berries, because of their bright colors, are high in antioxidants."

The biomedical scientist says such early research is exciting because many people would not associate such a sugary product with healthy biological properties.

"At this point, we are saying, if you choose to put syrup on your pancakes, it may be healthier to use real maple syrup," he said.

Seeram acknowledges that real maple syrup is more expensive than commercial brands with maple flavoring or even those with no or very little maple syrup. "But you pay for what you get and you get what you pay for, meaning there are consequences for what you eat . . . In a certain sense, people view sap as the lifeblood of the tree," Seeram said. "Maple syrup is unique in that it is the only commercial product in our diet that comes from a plant's sap."

Huevos Rancheros

These south of the boredom eggs are not just restaurant fare, they're easy to make at home. Ranch-style eggs with soft-fried corn tortillas are a popular way to start the day at many Mexican cafés and cantinas. Customize this dish with your choice of garnish. Look for canned chipotles in adobo sauce—which will keep after opening, covered, in the refrigerator (see page 65)—and queso or fresh Mexican cheese at grocery stores that stock Hispanic products.

Serves 4 • Prep Time: 10 minutes • Cook Time: 10 minutes

1   (15-ounce) can **black beans**, rinsed and drained

1   canned **chipotle** in adobo sauce, finely chopped

1   tablespoon **grapeseed oil** or **canola oil**

4   fresh (6-inch) corn tortillas

4   large **eggs**

1   cup prepared **tomato** salsa

½   cup chopped **green onions**

2   cups chopped fresh cilantro

½   cup chopped fresh **avocado**

½   cup crumbled queso, feta, or Monterey Jack cheese

    Lime wedges, for serving

1   In a saucepan, heat the black beans and chipotle over medium heat.

2   Heat the oil over medium-high heat in a large nonstick skillet. Fry the tortillas for about 10 seconds on each side or until warm. Drain on paper towels. Crack the eggs into the remaining oil and fry the eggs to your desired doneness.

3   To serve, place a warm tortilla on each plate and top each tortilla with 1 egg and 2 tablespoons each of salsa, green onions, cilantro, avocado, and cheese. Serve the black beans on the side, and pass the remaining salsa and lime wedges at the table.

Calories 421 • Total Fat 18g • Saturated Fat 5g • Carbohydrates 46g
Protein 21g • Dietary Fiber 15g • Sodium 938mg

WHO KNEW?

Q: What are the benefits of eating beans?

A: Research published in the November 2003 *Journal of Agriculture and Food Chemistry* indicates that black beans are as rich in antioxidant compounds, called anthocyanins, as grapes and cranberries, fruits long considered antioxidant superstars.

When researchers analyzed different types of beans, they found that the darker the bean's seed coat, the higher its level of antioxidant activity. Gram for gram, black beans were found to have the most antioxidant activity, followed in descending order by red, brown, yellow, and white beans.

Overall, the level of antioxidants found in black beans in this study is approximately ten times that found in an equivalent amount of oranges.

WHO KNEW?

Q: How do I buy chipotles in adobo sauce?

A: Chipotles are dried smoked jalapeños. Any Mexican or Latin food market will have them, and many supermarkets carry chipotles in adobo in their Hispanic food sections. The chipotles are soft and ready to go straight from the can. They can be quite spicy, but the heat can be tempered a bit by scraping out the seeds. Adobo refers to the tangy, slightly sweet red sauce. They are sold together in a can as a versatile pantry staple.

Use just the chipotles for intense smoky chile heat or just the sauce for a sour-sweet flavor and a slightly less fiery smoky heat. Transfer the unused chiles and sauce to an airtight container—preferably glass, as the sauce tends to stain plastic—and refrigerate for several months. Or try freezing individual chiles in an ice cube tray and then transfer the cubes to a sealable freezer bag. Frozen, they'll keep for about three months.

Bountiful Breakfast Strata

Some say that this Italian dish of multiple savory layers of eggs and cheese was named after the 1956 Fellini film *La Strada*, staring Anthony Quinn. This will be the dish that everyone asks you to bring to the family brunch. Assemble the night before the event, pop in the oven in the morning, and enjoy to rave reviews. But if you want to enjoy your strata within a couple of hours, our recipe helps you do that, too. Save and refrigerate any leftovers for breakfast or lunch the next day.

Serves 8 • Prep Time: 20 minutes • Cook Time: 55 minutes

12 ounces **turkey** or soy-based breakfast sausage

½ cup chopped **onion**

½ cup chopped red or yellow **bell pepper**

½ cup sliced **mushrooms**

2 cups low-fat **milk**

2 cups **egg whites**

3 large **eggs**

1 tablespoon Dijon mustard

½ teaspoon dried **oregano**

¾ teaspoon salt

½ teaspoon ground black pepper

4 cups cubed Whole Wheat and **Flaxseed** Boule (page 120), Whole Wheat and **Flaxseed** Baguettes (page 119), or other bread

¾ cup grated **Asiago cheese** (3 ounces)

1 Coat a nonstick skillet with a small amount of butter or oil and heat over medium-high heat. Cook the sausage, crumbling with a wooden spoon, for about 5 minutes, until cooked through. Stir in the onion, bell pepper, and mushrooms and cook, stirring, for about 5 minutes, until the vegetables are soft. Set aside.

2 In a bowl, whisk the milk, egg whites, eggs, mustard, oregano, salt, and pepper together until well blended.

3 To assemble, coat a large 3-quart casserole dish with a small amount of butter or oil and arrange the cubed bread on the bottom. Spoon the sausage mixture on top of the bread. Pour the egg mixture over all and sprinkle with the cheese. Bake right away or cover and refrigerate overnight.

4 To bake, preheat the oven to 350°F. Bake, covered, for 30 minutes. Remove the cover and bake for 15 minutes longer, or until lightly browned and set. Let stand for 10 minutes before serving.

Calories 220 • Total Fat 12g • Saturated Fat 5g • Carbohydrates 6g
Protein 23g • Dietary Fiber 0.5g • Sodium 450mg

WHO KNEW?

Q: Why all the fuss about flaxseed?

A: The research on flax has put it on the map, thanks to these three ingredients that flax contains: 1) omega-3 essential fatty acids for heart-healthy effects and inhibiting tumor incidence and growth; 2) lignans, which help protect against cancer by blocking enzymes that are involved in hormone metabolism, and by interfering with the growth and spread of tumor cells; and 3) fiber to help the digestion process.

DID YOU HEAR THE NEWS?

Grab your walking shoes and smile.

As noted in the April 20, 2011, edition of *USA Today*, "There is a growing body of research showing that exercise not only helps with the side effects of [cancer] treatment but also decreases the recurrence risk and improves overall survival," says researcher Melinda Irwin, an associate professor of epidemiology and public health at Yale University School of Medicine and principal investigator of the Yale Exercise and Survivorship study.

"Irwin says the verdict is still out on how exercise benefits cancer survivors, but she notes studies in which breast cancer survivors who exercise have lower levels of insulin, and some studies have shown that high levels of insulin strongly increase the risk for breast cancer recurrence and death."

The *Journal of Clinical Oncology* first reported the findings of Irwin's study in August 2008. Irwin says, "We not only showed an improvement in survival from breast cancer but survival from other causes such as cardiovascular disease and diabetes, so exercise is really associated with a multitude of benefits."

Wake-Up Pizza

Make this the night before, so it's ready to warm and savor when you wake up. Modeled after a breakfast pizza at Whole Foods Market, this one features a good-for-you crust and ingredients you might find in an omelet. And there's no zingy tomato sauce to startle your taste buds this early in the day. It's a carpool or in-flight dream meal; no need to heat, just eat. For a time-saver, pick the vegetables from the grocery store salad bar, wash thoroughly, and proceed with the recipe.

Serves 4 . . . or 1 hungry person • Prep Time: 10 minutes • Cook Time: 15 to 20 minutes

¼ cup cornmeal, for sprinkling

1 pound Whole Wheat and **Flaxseed** Dough (page 116) or prepared whole wheat pizza dough, or 1 prepared whole wheat pizza crust

All-purpose flour for dusting

1 tablespoon **olive oil**

1 tablespoon milled **flaxseed**

1 cup chopped **green onions**, with some green

1 cup thinly sliced red, green, and/or yellow **bell pepper** strips

1 cup thinly sliced **mushrooms**

1 cup thawed frozen or drained canned **artichoke** hearts, chopped

1 cup finely chopped **kale**, **Swiss chard**, or baby **spinach**

1 cup shredded aged **Gouda** or **Parmesan cheese** (about 4 ounces)

1 Preheat the oven to 450°F. Sprinkle a baking sheet with cornmeal.

2 Place the dough on a floured surface, dust the top with flour, and roll or pat into a 12-inch oval. Transfer the dough to the prepared pan, then re-form it into an oval. Brush the olive oil over the crust and dust with the milled flaxseed. Top the crust with the green onions, bell pepper strips, mushrooms, artichoke hearts, and kale, then sprinkle on the cheese.

3 Bake for 15 to 20 minutes, until the edges of the crust and the cheese are brown. Transfer the flatbread to a cutting board, cut into pieces, and serve.

Calories 197 • Total Fat 8g • Saturated Fat 4g • Carbohydrates 19g
Protein 14g • Dietary Fiber 5g • Sodium 573mg

Feel the benefits of bioenergy healing.

According to Laura Mead, Certified Bodywork Therapist and bioenergy practitioner, bioenergy healing is the practice of transferring life force from one person to another in order to benefit that person. This transfer of energy can aid an individual's physical, emotional, and mental states. Mead cites research by Juliann G. Kiang, John A. Ives, and Wayne B. Jonas, published in the journal *Molecular and Cellular Biochemistry* in March 2005 as an example of the ongoing studies involved in bioenergy and healing.

WOULD SOMEONE JUST TELL ME . . .

Q: I love that these foods have a positive impact on my immune system, healthy cells, muscle and joint function, bones, and heart health. But don't I need to boost my health with high doses of supplements?

A: Incorporating a wide variety of foods, preferably fresh ones in season, will naturally enrich your body with the nutrients it needs to maintain a strong immune system and fight off disease.

Researchers tend to focus on certain nutrients in breast cancer prevention. They include omega-3 fatty acids, vitamin D, and calcium, as you are reading about throughout this book. This book is full of recipes that include foods that contain these nutrients, and we like them because they also taste fantastic! And our book contains research that demonstrates populations who have healthy levels of these nutrients in their blood and diets have a lower risk of breast cancer and a better prognosis if they do get it. That said, we eat *food*, not individual nutrients. Studies have shown that high doses of supplements, as a general rule, do *not* protect against cancer. See your own health care practitioner for your individual nutritional needs.

Massage . . . not just a feel-good story.

Now it's official: People who undergo massage demonstrated measurable changes in their immune and endocrine response, according to findings of a study in the Cedars-Sinai Department of Psychiatry and Behavioral Neurosciences, published in the October 2010 issue of the *Journal of Alternative and Complementary Medicine*. In addition, randomized controlled trials have demonstrated that massage reduces pain and anxiety.

"This research indicates that massage doesn't only feel good, it also may be good for you," said Mark Rapaport, MD, the study's principal investigator. "More research is ahead of us but it appears that a single massage may deliver a measurable benefit."

Deep tissue massage is not advised during active treatment, according to Jennifer Klemp, PhD, MPH, managing director of the University of Kansas Breast Cancer Survivorship Center. She recommends following these precautions from the American Cancer Society before receiving a massage:

- Get approval from your health care provider before receiving a massage.

- Receive a massage only from a trained professional who has experience in the special considerations necessary after breast cancer surgeries and treatment.

- Be aware that some cancer survivors who have had radiation may find even a light touch on the treatment area to be uncomfortable.

- If you have allergic reactions to lotions or oils used during massage, this tendency can be increased after receiving radiation treatment.

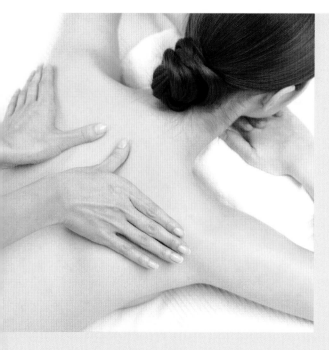

Compassionate Care

It's helpful to have a compassionate and caring person focused on making you feel relaxed and reconnected to yourself, and more connected to your body. I cannot emphasize enough the importance of taking these two steps before getting a massage: Receive permission from your health care provider, and work with a trained professional who has experience with massage for breast cancer survivors.

By Jennifer Shideler, LMT

Here's a brief case history: "Cathy" comes in for the first time after finishing her last chemotherapy treatment and getting the go-ahead from her doctor to have a massage. She has been told that her tissues and her lymph nodes are clean of cancer. She has physical scars on her chest from the several surgeries that she's had over the years that it's taken to fight the breast cancer battle. Her hair is still growing back, so she is wearing a sassy wig that looks like her own hair.

I could tell she felt awkward, self-conscious, and perhaps a little uneasy about lying on my table and being in public without her hair. I explain that I am working the cells through her body, but she can be at *ease* to be free of *disease*. I say that it's just the two of us in this dimly lit room; it's not her wig or her breasts that make her beautiful, it's her strength and courage that brought her into my office.

I suppose that having someone (a virtual stranger) touch you in such a caring, loving way after such a fight is a transition, but an important one. The muscles have memory beyond being accustomed to being overstretched or overshortened. They also remember trauma. Although Cathy may feel or think she has worked out all of the emotional scarring from her trauma, the muscles have their own healing cycle. It may take years. Be patient and kind to yourself, I tell her. Don't miss the benefit that massage can provide in the "back in the swing" process.

Jennifer Shideler is a specialist in therapeutic massage. She has focused on areas of recovery after illness to help people improve mood, increase relaxation and flexibility, and experience a mind-body connection while decreasing anxiety, respiration, and heart rate.

Strange how a teapot can represent at the same time the comforts of solitude and the pleasures of company.

~Author unknown

CHAPTER THREE
Beverages

Cool and Calm

*Try as we might, we can't control other people and
the things they do, but we can control what we do.
Our power always resides inside ourselves, so we
can use that power to control our thoughts, and
consequently, how those thoughts make us feel.*

~*Anonymous*

Think of beverages as inspirational "watering." Nothing beats water for simple,

healthy refreshment. Of course, you can drop in a few slices of fresh fruit or

cucumbers for a dash of flavor. But when you want something with a little

more zip, try these simple ways to hydrate and soothe the soul by mixing

some new flavors in with some old standbys. Juice, coffee, and tea have met

their soul mates in these liquid love matches!

Fresh Ginger Tea
with Honey and Lemon

Mmmmmmm! When you take a sip of this sweet escape in a cup, it will elicit this reaction. Fresh ginger has been used for centuries as an herbal remedy for stimulating the circulation and helping high blood pressure. It has also been used to treat respiratory conditions such as coughs, colds, and flu with its warming, soothing properties. So, sip this tea hot or cold. It's easy to make for yourself or for a friend in need of a little comfort. Our ginger tea gets more gingery the longer it steeps and is great for the sniffles, an upset stomach, a case of the "blahs," or whenever you need a liquid hug.

Makes 2 cups; serves 2 • Prep Time: 5 minutes • Cook Time: 5 minutes

2   inches fresh **ginger**, thinly sliced, or 2 tablespoons ground ginger

2   cups water

    Fresh **lemon juice** and **honey**

1   Bring the ginger and water to a boil in a saucepan over medium-high heat. Remove from the heat, cover, and let steep for 5 minutes.

2   Strain into cups or glasses, and add lemon juice, then honey to taste.

Calories 53 • Total Fat 0.5g • Saturated Fat 0g • Carbohydrates 13g
Protein 0.5g • Dietary Fiber 1g • Sodium 2mg

WHO KNEW?

Q: Where do I buy fresh ginger?

A: This might be the first time that you've bought fresh ginger at the grocery store. Check it out in the produce department. Whenever possible, choose fresh ginger over the dried form of the spice. It is not only superior in flavor but contains higher levels of gingerol. When selecting, make sure it is firm, smooth, and free of mold. Since it is sold by the pound, you can snap off a fat finger, if that's all you want.

Ginger comes in two forms, young or mature. Mature ginger, the more widely available type, has a tough skin that requires peeling; young ginger, available in Asian markets, does not need to be peeled.

Ginger Snaps You Back to Health

Preliminary laboratory experiments by the University of Michigan funded by the National Center for Complementary and Alternative Medicine, and reported in April 2006, suggest that gingerol, the active phytonutrient in ginger and the one responsible for its unique flavor, may have cancer-fighting properties. Ginger extracts have been shown to have antioxidant, anti-inflammatory, and antitumoral effects on cells. In another study, gingerol showed promise in managing nausea, a common side effect of cancer treatment.

What exactly is "chemo brain"?

Difficulty with cognitive function, commonly referred to as "chemo brain," is one of the side effects of chemotherapy, hormone therapy, immunotherapy, radiation, and surgery. Chemo brain includes: difficulty concentrating, mental fogginess, difficulty remembering details like conversations and recalling images, difficulty learning new skills and multitasking, taking longer to complete tasks, exhaustion, and being unusually disorganized.

Experts at the Mayo Clinic report that no medications have been proven to treat the effects of chemo brain. Some drugs that have been used to treat attention-deficit/hyperactivity disorder, Alzheimer's, and sleep problems can be prescribed to help lessen the effects.

According to the American Cancer Society, some simple ways to manage chemo brain, and to keep the brain performing at the highest levels, include doing simple tasks such as setting a daily routine, using a planner, getting enough rest and exercise, learning new skills, and even doing puzzles. (http://www.cancer.org/Treatment/TreatmentsandSideEffects/PhysicalSideEffects/ChemotherapyEffects/chemo-brain)

Chamomile and Apple Peel Tea

Just holding a warm cup of this tea and inhaling its sweet fragrance can make your body feel as happy as your mouth. Any chamomile tea will work, but organic chamomile with lavender from Traditional Medicinals puts more ingredients to work for you. Eat a peeled apple earlier in the day; cover and refrigerate the peel, then use it later for this tea. The soothing tea is sweetly calming and is great to drink an hour or so before bed.

Makes 2 cups; serves 2 • Prep Time: 5 minutes
Cook Time: 5 minutes

2   cups water

2   chamomile with **lavender** tea bags

    Peel of 1 small **apple**, preferably organic

    Fresh **lemon juice**

1   Bring the water to a boil in a saucepan over medium-high heat. Remove from the heat, add the tea bags and apple peel, cover, and steep for 5 minutes.

2   Strain into cups or glasses, and add the lemon juice to taste.

Calories 9 • Total Fat 0g • Saturated Fat 0g • Carbohydrates 3g • Protein 0g
Dietary Fiber 1.5g • Sodium 3mg

To lift or not to lift?

In the past, breast cancer survivors have been told not to lift weights for fear of developing lymphedema, the buildup of lymph fluid in the fatty tissues just under the skin of the arm, breast, and chest. Lymphedema is a possible side effect of surgery and radiation therapy. The swelling that results is more common in women who have had radiation therapy and many lymph nodes removed. Today, the risk of lymphedema is lower because of advances in patient care, including the sentinel lymph node biopsy, a procedure that removes fewer than five lymph nodes that are the first nodes, closest to the breast.

A study published in the *New England Journal of Medicine* in August 2009, "Weight Lifting in Women with Breast-Cancer-Related Lymphedema," found that "in breast cancer survivors with lymphedema, slowly progressive weight lifting had no significant effect on limb swelling and resulted in a decreased incidence of exacerbations of lymphedema, reduced symptoms, and increased strength."

In addition, a December 2010 edition of the *Journal of the American Medical Association* (JAMA) noted that the "findings of our study remove concerns that slowly progressive weight lifting will increase risk of lymphedema onset in breast cancer survivors. The many health benefits of weight lifting should now become available to all breast cancer survivors."

It may be helpful to seek advice when starting a weight-lifting program to understand physical limitations or risk of lymphedema.

Try to avoid muscle strain.

If you've had surgery or radiation treatment, ask your doctor or nurse when you can start to exercise and what type of exercises you can do. But keep in mind that overuse, which can result in injury, has been linked with the start of lymphedema in some women. It's a good idea to follow these tips:

- Use your affected arm as normally as you can. Once you are fully healed, about four to six weeks after surgery or radiation treatment, you can begin to go back to the activities you did before your surgery.

- Exercise regularly but try not to overtire your shoulder and arm. Before doing any strenuous exercise, such as lifting weights or playing tennis, talk with your doctor, nurse, or physical therapist. They can help you set goals and limits so that you can work at the level of activity that is right for you. Ask your doctor or physical therapist if you should be fitted for a sleeve to wear during strenuous activities.

- If your arm starts to ache, lie down and raise it above the level of your heart.

- Avoid vigorous, repeated activities, heavy lifting, or pulling.

- Use your unaffected arm or both arms as much as possible to carry heavy packages, groceries, handbags, or children.

The guidelines above are included in *Lymphedema: What Every Woman With Breast Cancer Should Know*, a booklet from the American Cancer Society. To download the report, including more instruction on how to prevent and control lymphedema, go to cancer.org/treatment.

Strawberry Agua Fresca: Fruit and Water!

A gentle soul lift for the spirit, fresh strawberries make a deliciously tart south-of-the-border fresh fruit beverage. Serve this drink in a large pitcher with lots of ice.

Makes about 4 cups; serves 4 • Prep Time: 5 minutes

2½ cups **strawberries**, hulled and rinsed

1½ cups sparkling spring or distilled water

3 tablespoons fresh lime juice

2 tablespoons **honey**, **agave nectar**, or **sorghum**

1 Place the strawberries and sparkling water in a blender or food processor and puree until smooth. Strain the juice into a pitcher. Stir in the lime juice, then add 2 tablespoons sweetener, or to taste. Serve over ice in tall glasses.

Calories 65 • Total Fat 17g • Saturated Fat 0g • Carbohydrates 17g
Protein 1g • Dietary Fiber 2g • Sodium 2mg

WHO KNEW?

Q: What makes strawberries so nutritious?

A: Not many foods offer more benefits: vitamin C, folate, anthocyanin, quercetin, and kaempferol (a few of the many flavonoids in strawberries with excellent antioxidant properties) together form an excellent team to fight cancer. Strawberries can neutralize the effect of oxidants that affect the brain, and because they are rich in iodine they can help provide for proper functioning of the brain and nervous system. Strawberries are also rich in potassium and magnesium content, both of which are very effective in lowering high blood pressure caused by sodium. With their high fiber, folate, no fats, and high antioxidants, strawberries form an ideal cardiac health pack, as they effectively reduce cholesterol.

I never felt I left living behind and continued to live normally, when physically able. When everything was over and the effects of the chemo/radiation had dissipated, especially the fatigue, and my body had adjusted to the oral medication I started, then I was really, totally back in the swing.

~Karin Lichterman, community volunteer

Cranberry-Raspberry Green Tea

Scientists continue to investigate new mechanisms that may establish cranberries and green tea as anticancer agents. Look for a no sugar–added, 100 percent cranberry-raspberry juice blend that also contains other good stuff: vitamins A, C, and E, as well as ginseng, such as the Langers brand. You can also substitute brewed ginseng tea for green in this recipe, for example, or another type of tea to suit your taste.

Makes 2 cups; serves 2 • Prep Time: 5 minutes

1 cup brewed **green tea** or **ginseng tea**

1 cup **cranberry-raspberry juice** with ginseng

1 Combine the tea and juice. Keep chilled until ready to serve.

Calories 81 • Total Fat 0g • Saturated Fat 0g • Carbohydrates 20g • Protein 0g
Dietary Fiber 0g • Sodium 6mg

CHAMOMILE AND APPLE PEEL TEA
(PAGE 79)

ORANGE-SCENTED HOT CHOCOLATE

Orange-Scented Hot Chocolate

Doesn't the sound of almond milk and chocolate sound like pure heaven? This special hot chocolate has that thick, creamy body that warms you up any day of the week . . . for comfort and a treat that is ready in a jiffy.

Makes 2 cups; serves 2 • Prep Time: 2 minutes • Cook Time: 3 minutes

2   cups vanilla-flavored **almond milk**

¼   cup unsweetened **cocoa powder**

¼   teaspoon salt

2   tablespoons packed light **brown sugar**

1   teaspoon freshly grated **orange zest**

Miniature marshmallows and curling thin strips of orange peel, for garnish (optional)

1 In a saucepan, whisk the almond milk, cocoa powder, salt, and brown sugar until well blended. Bring to a boil over medium-high heat. Remove from the heat and whisk in the orange zest.

2 Serve each cup topped with marshmallows and an orange peel, if you like.

Calories 205 • Total Fat 1g • Saturated Fat 0.3g • Carbohydrates 42g Protein 9g • Dietary Fiber 0.3g • Sodium 460mg

Secret Ingredient Smoothie

Shhhh! Don't tell anyone the secret ingredients in this anytime smoothie. Baby spinach and whey protein concentrate are hidden away in the fruity blend. Choose fruit according to your preference, making sure the amounts equal the recipe. Not everyone has frozen dark cherries on hand, but that doesn't mean you should ignore this delicious drink that yields at least two vegetable or fruit servings and lots of protein in each glass. Whey protein concentrate is available in the organic or health food section from makers like Bob's Red Mill, which can be purchased at Target, Safeway, or Whole Foods Market, just to name a few sources. When your bananas ripen a little too much—and there's always at least one that gets too ripe to eat as is—freeze them unpeeled. Then peel, chunk, and use in this smoothie.

Makes about 1 cup; serves 2 • Prep Time: 5 minutes

2   cups fresh baby **spinach**, stems removed

1   cup fresh or thawed frozen **blueberries**

1   large ripe **banana**

¼   cup chopped fresh or canned **pineapple**, with juice

½   cup fresh or thawed frozen dark sweet **cherries**

½   cup **orange juice**

¼   cup whey protein concentrate

    Fresh **blueberries** and diced **pineapple,** for garnish

1   Combine the spinach, blueberries, banana, pineapple, cherries, orange juice, and whey in a blender or food processor, and process until creamy. Pour into cups, garnish, and serve.

Calories 436 • Total Fat 1g • Saturated Fat 0g • Carbohydrates 52g
Protein 56g • Dietary Fiber 6g • Sodium 158mg

WHO KNEW?

Q: What is the difference between almond milk and soy milk?

A: Almond milk is made from finely ground almonds mixed with water and sometimes sugar (some brands make both sweetened and unsweetened varieties). Like soy milk and rice milk, almond milk is mostly water by weight. Almond milk has a thin consistency that takes some getting used to, but many people prefer its mild nutty taste and think it's less chalky than other plant-based milks. It is a popular choice for individuals with milk and/or soy allergies, people who are lactose-intolerant, and vegetarians and vegans. Though it is a heart-healthy choice, almond milk contains only one gram of protein per cup, which is significantly less than cow's milk or soy milk. Most brands are fortified with calcium and vitamin D, but you'll need to check the nutrition facts panel to be sure.

Traditional soy milk is made from pressed mature soybeans mixed with water and typically some sugar or sweetener to mask the slightly bitter taste of the unsweetened soy milk. Consult with your health care provider for your own personal recommended daily amount of soy.

Soy is the most popular "milk" choice for individuals who are lactose-intolerant, follow a vegan or vegetarian diet that doesn't include dairy, or have an allergy to cow's and other mammalian milks. Soy milk is naturally low in saturated fat, and because it's plant based, it's cholesterol free. It also offers up some nutrients that cow's milk does not, including heart-healthy omega-3 fats.

On the flip side, most brands of soy milk contain fewer grams of protein than cow's milk (and flavored soy milks typically contain even less protein than plain). Soy milk contains some natural calcium, but not nearly as much as cow's milk. However, most manufacturers fortify their soy milk products with calcium, vitamin D, and other nutrients found in cow's milk, so they end up having a very similar nutritional profile. The average plain or vanilla soy milk contains 100 to 140 calories per cup, a bit more than skim cow's milk. Light versions that contain fewer calories (50 to 90 calories per cup) and less fat are also available, but be aware that they also contain less protein.

Homemade Chocolate Syrup

Making your own chocolate syrup takes just a few minutes, but the benefits are many. First, it tastes fabulous. Second, you know exactly what's in it. And third, a little chocolate just makes any dish seem special. Stir this into coffee, drizzle it over fruit, or dip whole strawberries in it. Warm it up or serve it at room temperature. The no-fat, dark chocolate satisfies your chocolate craving, with a side of antioxidants.

Makes about 1 cup; serves 16 • Prep Time: 5 minutes • Cook Time: 10 minutes

½   cup unsweetened **cocoa** powder

¾   cup sugar

⅛   teaspoon salt

¾   cup water

1   teaspoon vanilla extract

1 Whisk the cocoa powder, sugar, and salt together in a small saucepan. Whisk in the water and bring to a boil over medium-high heat.

2 Cook, whisking, for 2 to 3 minutes, until the sugar dissolves and the syrup is smooth. Stir in the vanilla. The syrup will thicken as it cools. Store, covered, in the refrigerator.

Calories 40 • Total Fat 0.5g • Saturated Fat 0g • Carbohydrates 11g
Protein 0.5g • Dietary Fiber 1g • Sodium 20mg

Research on pets and spouses— who is more beneficial to our health?

Pets aren't only cuddly and lovable . . . they are good for your heart, too. Researcher Karen Allen and colleagues at the State University of New York at Buffalo, found that pet owners have significantly lower resting blood pressure and heart rate compared to non–pet owners. The research study, published in September 1, 2002, in *Psychosomatic Medicine*, reported that individuals had the smallest increases in heart responses to stress if they had a pet in the room with them, and they recovered from stress faster. Pets were even better stress reducers than spouses. Give that fluffy heart medicine a hug today!

WHO KNEW?

Q: Are all forms of chocolate created equal?

A: In addition to having antioxidant qualities, research indicates that flavanols found in cocoa and chocolate have other positive influences on vascular health, such as lowering blood pressure and improving blood flow to the brain and heart, and lowering cholesterol.

But not all forms of chocolate contain high levels of flavanols. The more chocolate is processed, as are most commercially sold chocolates, the more flavanols are lost. Although it was once believed that dark chocolate contained the highest levels of flavanols, recent research indicates that, depending on how the dark chocolate was processed, this may not be true. The good news is that most major chocolate manufacturers are looking for ways to keep the flavanols in their processed chocolates, some noting their flavanol content on their packaging.

According to preliminary research at the Cleveland Clinic, in March 2010, your best choices now are dark chocolate over milk chocolate and cocoa powder that has not undergone Dutch processing.

AZTEC GUACAMOLE (PAGE 108)

POMEGRANATE
SPARKLER

Pomegranate Sparkler

Who says you have to sacrifice fizz for good health? You don't want to or have to, and this recipe proves it. Like a wine spritzer or grown-up Shirley Temple . . . this recipe makes one of the healthiest juices on mother earth glisten. Hot or cold, this drink quenches your thirst, revives your spirits, nourishes your body, and helps fight the aging process.

Makes 2 cups; serves 4 • Prep Time: 5 minutes

2   cups **pomegranate juice**, chilled

1   tablespoon **honey**, **agave nectar**, or **sorghum**

    Sparkling water, chilled

    Slice or twist of lime, for garnish

1   Pour the pomegranate juice into a pitcher. Add 1 tablespoon sweetener, or to taste, and stir to blend. Cover and keep in the refrigerator until ready to serve.

2   To serve, pour ½ cup pomegranate juice into a juice glass (or champagne glass for a fancier toast!) and top up with sparkling water. Add a lime twist and serve.

Calories 84 • Total Fat 0g • Saturated Fat 0g • Carbohydrates 21g • Protein 0g
Dietary Fiber 0g • Sodium 12mg

The Surprising Power of the Pomegranate

According to a laboratory study using cell cultures and animal models reported in the January 2010 issue of *Cancer Prevention Research*, eating pomegranates or drinking pomegranate juice may help prevent and slow the growth of some types of breast cancer, because of the phytochemicals that they contain. And pomegranates are being studied as a functional food for humans, based on this and other research.

Scientists don't know yet what amount of pomegranate juice a person would have to drink to receive the benefit. What they do know is that the ellagitannins in pomegranates work by inhibiting aromatase, a key enzyme used by the body to make estrogen; aromatase plays a key role in breast cancer growth.

"Phytochemicals suppress estrogen production that prevents the proliferation of breast cancer cells and the growth of estrogen-responsive tumors," according to researcher Shiuan Chen, PhD, director of the Division of Tumor Cell Biology and coleader of the Breast Cancer Research Program at City of Hope in Duarte, California. "We were surprised by our findings," Chen says. "We previously found other fruits, such as grapes, to be capable of the inhibition of aromatase. But phytochemicals in pomegranates and in grapes are different."

Leaving the scientists to finish their studies, we support enjoying pomegranate juice because it tastes great!

I was starting to report on more feature stories at work, by far my favorite type of reporting, and I spent more time thinking about day-to-day things and less about cancer.

Roz Varon, television anchor/reporter

Sea Breeze Mocktail

So easy and good, this recipe provides a new rounded smoothness, due to the vanilla. Look for a no sugar—added cranberry juice and squeeze several pink grapefruits to get the freshest juice. For an extra festive touch, use a fresh sprig of rosemary as a swizzle stick.

Makes 3 cups; serves 3 • Prep Time: 5 minutes

2 cups **cranberry juice**, preferably no sugar added

1 cup fresh or bottled unsweetened pink **grapefruit juice** (from 3 to 4 grapefruits)

½ teaspoon vanilla extract

Honey, **agave nectar**, or **sorghum**

1 Combine the cranberry and grapefruit juices. Add ½ teaspoon vanilla, or to taste. If you prefer, add a little sweetener. Serve on ice or chilled.

Calories 124 • Total Fat 0g • Saturated Fat 0g • Carbohydrates 30g
Protein 0.5g • Dietary Fiber 0.5g • Sodium 4mg

Mocha Grande

There's no need to leave home to drink your own specialty coffee at a fraction of the store-bought price.

Serves 1 • Prep Time: 5 minutes

1½ cups freshly brewed **coffee**

2 tablespoons Homemade **Chocolate** Syrup (page 88)

¼ cup warm skim **milk** or 2% milk

1 Pour the hot coffee into a mug. Stir in the chocolate syrup until it is dissolved, then add ¼ cup milk, or to taste, and serve.

Calories 54 • Total Fat 0g • Saturated Fat 0g • Carbohydrates 5g
Protein 2.5g • Dietary Fiber 2g • Sodium 33mg

Viennese Spiced Coffee

Serves 1 • Prep Time: 5 minutes

2 tablespoons packed light **brown sugar**

½ teaspoon ground **cinnamon**

⅛ teaspoon freshly grated **nutmeg**

1½ cups freshly brewed **coffee**

1 Stir the brown sugar, cinnamon, and nutmeg together in a coffee mug. Top up with freshly brewed coffee, stir until the sugar dissolves, and enjoy.

Calories 113 • Total Fat 0g • Saturated Fat 0g • Carbohydrates 30g
Protein 0.5g • Dietary Fiber 2g • Sodium 15mg

I KNEW I WAS BACK IN THE SWING WHEN . . .

Being a breast cancer survivor was not top of my mind when I answered my own question of "Who am I?"

~Carol LaRue, author and occupational therapist

WHO KNEW?

Q: Coffee may taste good and get you going in the morning, but what will it do for your health?

A: The September 2004 issue of *Harvard Women's Health Watch* reported on the vast majority of studies that have demonstrated the health benefits of coffee, including countering risk factors for diabetes, heart attack, and stroke.

Coffee has also been linked to lower risk of dementia, including Alzheimer's disease. A study from Finland and Sweden, published in the *Journal of Alzheimer's Disease* in January 2009, showed that, out of 1,400 people followed for about 20 years, those who reported drinking 3 to 5 cups of coffee daily were 65 percent less likely to develop dementia and Alzheimer's disease, compared with nondrinkers or occasional coffee drinkers. In addition, findings of a University of South Florida mouse study were published in the June 2011 *Journal of Alzheimer's Disease*. The results demonstrated that caffeinated coffee offers protection against the memory-robbing disease that is not possible with other caffeine containing drinks or decaffeinated coffee.

Finally, a study published in the May 17, 2011, online edition of the *Journal of the National Cancer Institute*, Harvard School of Public Health researchers found that men who regularly drink coffee appear to have a lower risk of developing a lethal form of prostate cancer. All the more reason to enjoy a cup of antioxidants with a side of spice! (see page 42).

Fresh Ginger Cider

Make extra for savoring while sitting on the porch and neighboring, taking in a little sunshine and Vitamin D at the same time. (Don't forget the sunscreen; dermatologists recommend no more than ten to fifteen minutes of unprotected sun exposure a day.) Served hot or cold, this drink quenches your thirst, revives your spirits, and nourishes your body. Not bad for a drink with only two ingredients. Pour it into a thermal container and take it with you tailgating, no matter what the weather, or to a friend who could use a little TLC, as this drink both invigorates and soothes.

Makes 4 cups; serves 4 • Prep Time: 5 minutes • Cook Time: 5 minutes

4   cups **apple juice** or **apple cider**

1   (3-inch) piece fresh unpeeled **ginger**, cut into thin rounds (see page 77)

1   Combine the apple juice and ginger in a saucepan over medium-high heat and bring to a simmer. Remove from the heat. Cover and let steep for 30 minutes.

2   Strain out the ginger, if you wish, before pouring the apple juice. Serve right away in mugs, or chill and serve in glasses over ice.

Calories 115 • Total Fat 0g • Saturated Fat 0g • Carbohydrates 28g
Protein 0g • Dietary Fiber 0.5g • Sodium 10mg

Let the music begin!

In just a few minutes of listening to music, many people are able to think more clearly and face the day with a more positive attitude.

"Many years of research have shown me that there is no set prescription, no particular piece of music that will make everyone feel better or more relaxed," says Suzanne Hanser, EdD, chairperson of the music therapy department at Berklee College of Music, and a music therapist at Dana-Farber Cancer Institute, both in Boston. "What counts is familiarity, musical taste, and the kinds of memories, feelings, and associations a piece of music brings to mind. The key is to individualize your musical selections."

THE TOP TEN HAPPY SONGS

The December 13, 2009, *Spin* magazine story, "Happiest, Saddest, Most Exhilarating Songs Ever," describes how British researchers determined the saddest, happiest, and most exhilarating tracks in music history. Dr. Harry Witchel used a list of songs compiled by the Official U.K. Charts Company to determine the "tune trigger quotient" of study participants by measuring heart rate, skin temperature, and breathing patterns. The Top Ten Happy Songs, according to the study:

1 Lily Allen "LDN"

2 ABBA "Dancing Queen"

3 R.E.M. "Shiny Happy People"

4 B52s "Love Shack"

5 Beatles "She Loves You"

6 Beyoncé "Crazy in Love"

7 Britney Spears "Baby One More Time"

8 Bill Medley and Jennifer Warnes "I've Had the Time of My Life"

9 Spice Girls "Spice Up Your Life"

10 Kylie Minogue "Spinning Around"

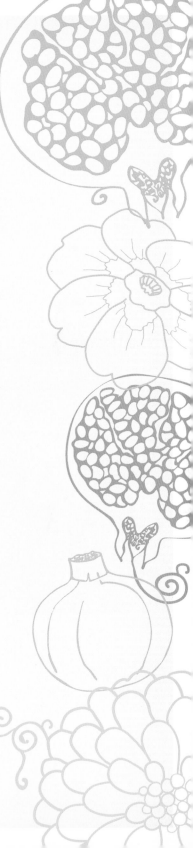

Nothing in life is to be feared.
It is only to be understood.

~Madame Curie

Appetizers and Snacks

Determined

"No bird soars too high, if he soars with his own wings."

~William Blake

To use a little poetic license with Shakespeare: An appetizer or snack by any other name would taste as delicious. Yes, these favorites full of flavor and treats from the garden are not only meant to be savored as appetizers or snacks, they also are our dish of choice for the main event at lunch or dinner. So don't let the chapter title define your daily fare—embrace each recipe when you feel the urge for a small plate with a large taste.

Black Bean, Tomato, and Corn Salsa with Baked Tortilla Chips

Here's the world's easiest salsa recipe. A day's serving of vegetables in one full scoop—this is the real deal. It's so vibrant, you will taste the difference between this delight and the sauce in a jar that's lost its zip of nutrients by sitting on the shelf and being stored in the dark—losing its light and energy-giving vibrancy.

Serves 12 • Prep Time: 10 minutes • Cook Time: 12 to 14 minutes • Refrigeration Time: 2 to 3 hours

BLACK BEAN, TOMATO, AND CORN SALSA

2   (15-ounce) cans **black beans**, rinsed and drained

1   (15-ounce) can corn, rinsed and drained

1   cup canned **tomatoes**, drained and chopped

1   cup finely chopped **red onion**

½   cup finely chopped green **bell pepper**

¼   cup chopped cilantro

2   cloves **garlic**, minced

½   teaspoon ground cumin

½   teaspoon sea salt

2   teaspoons **olive oil**, **grapeseed oil**, or **canola oil**

1   small jalapeño **chile**, seeded and finely diced

    Juice of 1 lime

BAKED TORTILLA CHIPS

12   (6-inch) corn tortillas

1   tablespoon **grapeseed oil** or **canola oil**

1   teaspoon kosher or sea salt

1   For the salsa, combine the black beans, corn, tomatoes, onion, green bell pepper, cilantro, garlic, cumin, salt, oil, chile, and lime juice in a large bowl and toss to blend. Cover and refrigerate for several hours to let the flavors blend.

2   For the chips, preheat the oven to 350°F. With a sharp knife or pizza wheel, cut each tortilla into 8 wedges. Arrange the wedges on 2 large baking sheets. Brush the tops with oil and sprinkle with salt.

3   Bake for 6 to 7 minutes, then rotate the trays in the oven. Continue baking for 6 to 7 minutes longer, until the chips are lightly browned. Serve right away or let cool, then store in an airtight container until ready to serve.

4   Serve the chips with a pair of salsas: this one and Fresh Pineapple Salsa (page 201).

Calories 207 • Total Fat 3.5g • Saturated Fat 0.5g • Carbohydrates 38g Protein 8.5g • Dietary Fiber 10g • Sodium 400mg

Bruschetta with Roasted Tomatoes and Garlic

You know those toasty little open-faced tomato-garlic sandwiches? Here they are in a homemade, fast, and fashionable recipe. Who knew they could be so good for you and so economical? They sound so exotic, but they truly are a basic staple of our real food redo. Brush baguette slices with a little olive oil and toast in the oven, then dollop on this colorful topping. Leftover roasted tomatoes are also great on a veggie burger or flatbread.

Serves 8 • Prep Time: 10 minutes • Cook Time: 25 to 30 minutes

2 loaves Whole Wheat and **Flaxseed** Baguettes (page 119) or store-bought whole grain baguettes, sliced

1 tablespoon **olive oil**, for brushing

ROASTED TOMATO, GARLIC, AND BASIL TOPPING

12 Roma **tomatoes**, halved lengthwise

4 cloves **garlic**, peeled

2 tablespoons **olive oil**

Salt and pepper

½ cup or 1 handful fresh **basil** leaves

½ cup coarsely chopped fresh Italian **parsley**, plus more for garnish

1 Preheat the oven to 400°F. Brush one side of each baguette slice with olive oil and place on a rimmed baking sheet.

2 Line a second rimmed baking sheet with aluminum foil. Toss the tomatoes, garlic, and olive oil together in a large bowl until the tomatoes glisten. Turn the tomato mixture out onto the second prepared pan and smooth into one layer. Season with salt and pepper.

3 Roast the tomatoes for 25 to 30 minutes, until softened and caramelized. Remove from the oven and let cool in the pan. During the last 10 minutes of roasting, toast the baguette slices in the oven until they brown around the edges, then remove from the oven and let cool in the pan.

4 When the tomatoes are cool enough to handle, remove and discard the skins and seeds. Place the roasted tomato pulp and garlic, and the basil and parsley, in a food processor or blender and pulse 8 times, or until coarsely chopped and blended. Taste for seasoning. To serve, top each slice with a spoonful of topping. Sprinkle each with Italian parsley.

Calories 61 • Total Fat 5g • Saturated Fat 1g • Carbohydrates 3.5g
Protein 1g • Dietary Fiber 1g • Sodium 4mg

Orange-Cranberry Chutney

This recipe puts the appetite back into appetizers, as you can simply eat this by the spoonful. Top Neufchâtel cheese with this chutney and serve with toasted baguette slices for an easy, good-for-you appetizer. Use it as a tangy counterpoint to roasted chicken and turkey or a veggie burger. And it makes a great holiday gift. Buy cranberries in season, then keep them in the freezer for use all year long.

Makes 3 cups or six-½-cup servings • Prep Time: 10 minutes • Cook Time: 15 minutes

12 ounces fresh **cranberries** (about 3 cups)

1 cup sweetened or unsweetened dried **cherries**

½ cup sweetened dried **cranberries** or Craisins®

1½ teaspoons ground **cinnamon**

½ teaspoon ground **ginger**

2 cloves **garlic**, minced

⅓ cup packed light **brown sugar**

Grated zest and juice of 2 **oranges**

¼ cup **apple cider vinegar**

1½ cups **apple juice** or **apple cider**

¼ teaspoon salt

1 Combine the fresh cranberries, dried cherries, dried cranberries, cinnamon, ginger, garlic, brown sugar, orange zest and juice, vinegar, apple juice, and salt in a large saucepan over medium heat and cook, stirring, for about 5 minutes, until the cranberries begin to pop. Reduce the heat to low and cook, stirring occasionally, for 10 minutes longer, or until the mixture has thickened. Cool and refrigerate, covered. The chutney should keep for several weeks in the refrigerator.

Calories 220 • Total Fat 0.5g • Saturated Fat 0g • Carbohydrates 50g
Protein 1g • Dietary Fiber 3.5g • Sodium 200mg

Roasted Red Pepper Hummus with Warm Pita Bread and Endive

Until you've had hummus this good, you haven't really hummus-ed! Here's the key—homemade is best. Most garbanzo beans found in grocery stores or salad bars (especially canned garbanzos) are the cream-colored, relatively round kabuli beans, another name for garbanzo beans or chickpeas. Just put the hummus ingredients in the blender or food processor, then warm the pita bread, and you're minutes away from nibbling.

Serves 8 • Prep Time: 5 minutes • Cook Time: 5 minutes

1   (15-ounce) can **garbanzo beans**, rinsed and drained (about 1½ cups)

2   cloves **garlic**, minced or pressed

⅓   cup fresh **lemon juice**

⅛   teaspoon ground cumin

⅓   cup tahini (**sesame** paste) or smooth peanut butter

⅓   cup jarred **roasted red peppers**, rinsed and drained

     Salt and pepper

¼   cup chopped fresh Italian **parsley**

8   small pita breads

     Olive oil or **grapeseed oil**, for brushing

4   small heads Belgian **endive**, trimmed and separated into leaves

1   For the hummus, combine the garbanzo beans, garlic, lemon juice, cumin, and tahini in a blender or food processor. Process until smooth. Add the red peppers and pulse, until the peppers are finely chopped. Add the salt and pepper to taste. Transfer to a serving bowl and garnish with the chopped parsley. The hummus can be made 1 day in advance. Cover and chill until ready to serve. Bring to room temperature before serving.

2   For the pita bread, brush the pita all over with oil, and broil or heat in a skillet on both sides until blistered and hot. When cool enough to handle, cut each pita into 8 triangles with kitchen shears or a sharp knife. Serve the hummus in a bowl, surrounded by pita triangles and endive leaves.

Calories 250 • Total Fat 8g • Saturated Fat 1g • Carbohydrates 38g
Protein 11g • Dietary Fiber 11g • Sodium 278mg

WHO KNEW?

Q: How do I press, slice, or mince fresh garlic?

A: **Pressed garlic:** When using a garlic press, place the garlic inside and squeeze hard until all the garlic is pressed through.

Sliced garlic: Use a sharp paring knife to make the slices as thin as possible.

Minced garlic: Once the garlic is sliced, you can then mince it. Use a chopping motion with the knife, holding down the tip. Carefully brush the garlic off your knife, as it tends to pile up on the knife as you continue to mince.

Go with garbanzos!

Garbanzo beans are perfect for your digestive support, especially if you are focusing on the colon. From 65 to 75 percent of the fiber found in garbanzo beans is insoluble fiber, which produces by-products in your colon that fuel cells in your intestines, keeping the colon working as designed.

A University of Illinois study, published in the March 2010 journal *Brain, Behavior, and Immunity*, demonstrates the benefits of soluble fiber because it reduces the inflammation associated with obesity-related diseases and strengthens the immune system. "Soluble fiber (found in oat bran, barley, nuts, seeds, lentils, citrus fruits, apples, strawberries, and carrots) changes the personality of immune cells. They go from being pro-inflammatory, angry cells to anti-inflammatory, healing cells that help us recover faster from infection," said Gregory Freund, a professor at the University of Illinois College of Medicine and a faculty member in the College of Agriculture, Consumer, and Environmental Sciences' Division of Nutritional Sciences.

Insoluble fiber—found in foods, such as whole wheat and whole grain products, wheat bran, and green, leafy vegetables—is also valuable for providing bulk and helping food move through the digestive system, but it doesn't provide the boost to the immune system that soluble fiber provides.

Attitude is everything. I convinced myself that cancer was a temporary inconvenience and that my personal strength was enough to get me through it. Cultivating that tough inner actress helped me believe that I could cope.

~Elaine Nelson, elementary school teacher

Aztec Guacamole

You won't believe how good this tastes until you leave the packaged treat behind. Before the Spanish arrived in Mexico, the Aztecs were making *āhuacamolli* with a stone mortar and pestle known as a *molcajete*. At some Mexican restaurants, that is still how it's made, tableside, where you can choose what you do and don't want added, as well. On a hot day, make this guacamole and the tortilla chips, then enjoy yourself with a Strawberry Agua Fresca (page 82) over ice. If you like more heat, seed only two of the chilies and include the seeds of the other one when you mix all the ingredients together. Baked Tortilla Chips will give you 2 tortillas (16 chips) per person.

Serves 6 • Prep Time: 15 minutes • Refrigeration Time: 30 minutes

1 medium ripe avocado, halved, pitted, and peeled

Juice of 1 **lemon**

1 clove **garlic**, minced

1 cup diced **tomato**

¼ cup chopped cilantro

¼ cup diced **red onion**

¼ teaspoon ground cumin

3 small jalapeño or serrano **chiles**, seeded and minced

Salt and pepper

Baked Tortilla Chips (page 102)

1 Mash the avocado in a large bowl. Add the lemon juice and mix with a fork. Add the garlic, tomato, cilantro, onion, cumin, and chiles. Mix well and season with the salt and pepper. Refrigerate for 30 minutes and serve with the chips.

Calories 51 • Total Fat 7g • Saturated Fat 0.5g • Carbohydrates 5g
Protein 1g • Dietary Fiber 2g • Sodium 4mg

WHO KNEW?

Q: How do you seed a chile?

A: Follow these three easy steps, courtesy of Cookthink.com:

Most of the heat in a chile pepper—whether jalapeño, serrano, habanero, or another—comes from the white ribs and seeds. Removing both seeds and ribs reduces the chile's heat and allows more of the pepper's flavor to come through.

First, cut the pepper in half lengthwise. If you want the halves to stay intact for larger slices or a large dice, just trim out the seeds and ribs, cut out the stem, and slice the pepper as thick or thin as you like.

It's easier to get the seeds and ribs out if you cut each half in half again.

To get the seeds and ribs out, hold each quarter by the end. With the knife parallel to the cutting board, slice across the ribs and seeds. When you get to the top of the pepper, turn the knife downward toward the cutting board and chop off the stem with the same motion.

WOULD SOMEONE JUST TELL ME . . .

Q: How can we start a Back in the Swing Cookbook Club?

A: Yes! Here are some ways to get started:

Show this book to your doctor or nurse and suggest getting an ongoing support group to implement a book club component. Each chapter of the book could be the guide to a breast cancer survivor group meeting, perhaps led by a nurse navigator, social worker, or other trained cancer survivorship expert.

Or focus on the nutrition lessons and create a weekly cooking night where friends use this cookbook for twelve weeks, led by a dietician and local foodie, both of whom could combine the fun of playing in the kitchen with skills to practice at home.

Seven Easy
Workout Recipes
for Each Day of the Week

Mary Fry, PhD, associate professor, specialist in sports and exercise psychology, the University of Kansas, and her graduate students suggest:

- Do **wall sits** while you strengthen your legs.

- Put on a high-tempo CD and do some **sit-ups** or **crunches** to the beat to strengthen your core.

- Do **arm stretches** to increase your range of motion.

- **Jump rope** . . . see how many you can do in one minute to strengthen your heart.

- **Run** up and down some steps, not carrying laundry, for more aerobics.

- Do **walking lunges** around the kitchen to strengthen your hamstrings.

- Do a **child's pose** to stretch your lower back.

WALL SIT

ARM STRETCHES

CHILD'S POSE

Thai Lettuce Cups

Crisp lettuce cups or endive leaves hold the tasty filling in these little bites. If you're packing these wraps to take on the road, keep the lettuce cups and the filling chilled and pack them separately. Make a batch of the filling, then use it over the course of several days to fill the lettuce leaves and enjoy for a casual meal or a snack. For faster preparation, cook ½ cup brown rice ahead of time; this should give you 1½ cups cooked rice in about 20 minutes.

Serves 4 • Prep Time: 10 minutes • Cook Time: 10 minutes

1   teaspoon **grapeseed oil** or **canola oil**

1   clove **garlic**, minced or pressed

1   small red serrano **chile**, seeded and finely chopped, or ¼ cup chopped red **bell pepper**

8   ounces ground **turkey**, ground **chicken**, or **tofu**

2   teaspoons nam pla (bottled Thai fish sauce) or Worcestershire sauce

1½ cups cooked **brown rice**

4   **green onions**, with some green, thinly sliced

½   cup light coconut milk

    Grated zest and juice of 1 lime

¼   cup chopped fresh cilantro

2   large heads **Belgian endive** or Little Gem lettuce (small heads of romaine), separated into leaves, rinsed, and patted dry

1   Heat the oil in a large nonstick skillet over medium-high heat. Sauté the garlic and chile for 2 minutes. Stir in the turkey and sauté for about 4 minutes, until cooked through. Transfer to a bowl and stir in the nam pla, brown rice, green onions, coconut milk, lime zest and juice, and cilantro. Stir to blend well. Cover and refrigerate until ready to serve.

2   To serve, mound a spoonful of filling in the curved part of each leaf and eat.

Calories 394 • Total Fat 9g • Saturated Fat 2g • Carbohydrates 59g
Protein 19g • Dietary Fiber 7g • Sodium 90mg

Spa Sushi

This spa version has all the flavor, minus the raw fish. At better grocery or health food stores, as well as Target, you can find sushi ingredients for this recipe, including: nori (dried seaweed sheets in cellophane packages), rice vinegar, pink pickled ginger, tamari sauce, wasabi paste (green Japanese horseradish), and even a small woven sushi mat to help you roll it all up. Adapted from a sushi served at Canyon Ranch spas, this sushi also includes brown rice for better nutrition. Just cook it a little longer than package directions suggest, until the rice sticks together.

Makes 16 pieces; serves 8 • Prep Time: 25 minutes • Cook Time: 20 minutes

1½ cups long-grain **brown rice**, cooked until sticky

2 tablespoons rice vinegar

4 **nori** sheets

1 cup shredded **carrot**

1 cup finely chopped cucumber

1 cup finely chopped red **bell pepper**

1 medium avocado, halved, pitted, peeled, and cut into 16 slices

Pickled ginger, **tamari sauce**, and prepared wasabi

1 In a bowl, combine the rice with the rice vinegar and stir with a fork to blend.

2 To assemble, place each nori sheet on a woven sushi mat. Dip your fingers in water and brush 1 nori sheet to moisten. Spread one-quarter of the rice mixture on the bottom two-thirds of the nori sheet, leaving a 1-inch perimeter on three sides. Arrange a row of carrot across the middle of the rice. Arrange a row of cucumber on top of the carrot, a row of bell pepper on top of the cucumber, and 4 slices of avocado on top of the bell pepper. Starting from the bottom, and using the sushi mat to help you grip the nori sheet, roll tightly and away from you until you have a cylinder. Place the cylinder, seam side down, on a flat surface and repeat the process with the remaining nori sheets, rice mixture, and fillings.

3 To serve, cut each cylinder into 4 pieces with a sharp knife. Serve, filling side up, with little bowls of ginger, tamari sauce, and wasabi.

Calories 114 • Total Fat 8g • Saturated Fat 3g • Carbohydrates 7g
Protein 4.5g • Dietary Fiber 0.5g • Sodium 48mg

I KNEW I WAS BACK IN THE SWING WHEN . . .

I was getting to that place where I felt that my body, mind, and spirit were my own, again. Not waking up every morning or going to sleep each night with the word cancer circling in my head. Feeling the strength to talk about what I've been through, and hoping that strength will help someone else who is going through some of the same things that I have experienced.

~Anonymous

WHO KNEW?

Q: What kind of olive oil should I buy and how do I store it?

A: "Virgin olive oil" denotes oil obtained from the fruit of the olive tree solely by mechanical or other means that cause no alteration or deterioration of the oil. No heat, no chemical interaction, no solvents, no radiation, no microwaves!

The best oils, those called "extra-virgin," are cold-pressed, a chemical-free process that involves only cold pressure or cold centrifugation, which produces a natural level of low acidity. Extra-virgin olive oils must have an acidity of less than 1 percent. Virgin olive oils, on the other hand, may have an acidity of 1 to 2 percent.

STORING: Olive oil should be stored in a closed container, away from heat or light. Correctly stored, good oil has a shelf life of twelve to eighteen months. You do not need to store oil in the refrigerator. However, if you do, it will turn cloudy but should still be fine—just leave it at room temperature for half an hour, and it will return to its previous consistency.

Oxygen may cause olive oil to become rancid. The rancidity starts from the surface where air exposure is continuous; bottle necks are narrow, so that the surface area exposed to air is minimized. When the remaining olive oil will not be used for a month or so, it is better to transfer the olive oil to a smaller container, fill it up halfway, and seal the lid tightly to prevent air penetration.

Roasted Rosemary Garbanzo Snacks

Finally! The snack that puts the potato chip in its place. It's so delicious you won't believe it's beans. Once you serve them, your book club won't let you in the door at the next meeting without these nutty-tasting, protein-rich treats.

Serves 2; makes 1½ cups • Prep Time: 5 minutes • Cook Time: 25 to 30 minutes

1 (15-ounce) can **garbanzo beans**, rinsed and drained, patted dry

1 tablespoon **olive oil**

1 tablespoon fresh **rosemary** leaves, or 1 teaspoon dried rosemary leaves

1 Preheat the oven to 400°F. In a medium bowl, gently toss the garbanzo beans with the olive oil and rosemary. Spread in a single layer on a rimmed baking sheet.

2 Bake for 25 to 30 minutes, turning the beans halfway through, until browned and crispy.

Calories 408 • Total Fat 12g • Saturated Fat 1.5g • Carbohydrates 58g Protein 19g • Dietary Fiber 5g • Sodium 300mg

PROFESSOR POSITIVE
Seeking Out the Silver Lining!

Benefit finding means finding the "silver lining" of a challenging or stressful life event. Many negative experiences can change people for the better, causing them to develop closer interpersonal relationships, a greater sense of meaning in life, and a strong sense of compassion and empathy for others. Strive to search for the positive impact of your life experiences. Not only will this make you feel better but it has also been shown to reduce symptoms and cancer-related doctor visits in those who engage in this activity, according to the June 2003 *Journal of Clinical Oncology*.

Whole Wheat and Flaxseed Dough

The no-knead dough in this recipe is mixed in a bowl and sits, covered, on your kitchen counter for 2 hours to rise; then, it can be used right away or stored in your refrigerator for up to 3 days before baking. Use a full recipe for bread—one larger round loaf (page 120) or 2 baguettes (page 119). Use one-half of the dough to make flatbread (page 117) or pizza (page 68). If you can make brownies from a mix, you can make this bread, but two things are important: 1) Measure the flours as the recipe states—scooping from the flour bag and dumping into the measuring cup. 2) Make sure to get fine-granulated instant or bread machine yeast that you can just stir into the flour.

Makes 2 pounds dough • Prep Time: 25 minutes

2¼ cups unbleached all-purpose or bread flour

1 cup whole wheat or white whole wheat flour

¼ cup milled **flaxseed**

1 tablespoon instant or bread machine yeast

¾ tablespoon kosher salt

¾ cup hot water

¾ cup cold water

1 Spoon the flour, whole wheat flour, and flaxseed into a measuring cup, level with a knife or your finger, then dump the flour into a large mixing bowl.

2 Add the yeast and salt to the flour. Stir together with a wooden spoon or Danish dough whisk. Combine the hot water and cold water in a 2-cup measuring cup. Pour the water into the flour mixture and stir together until just moistened. Beat 40 strokes, scraping the bottom and the sides of the bowl, until the dough forms a lumpy, sticky mass.

3 Cover the bowl with plastic wrap and let rise at room temperature (72°F) in a draft-free place for 2 hours, or until the dough has risen near the top of the bowl and has a sponge-like appearance.

4 Use right away or refrigerate the dough, covered, for up to 3 days before baking.

Calories 70 • Total Fat 0.5g • Saturated Fat 0g • Carbohydrates 15g
Protein 2g • Dietary Fiber 1.5g • Sodium 220mg

Greek Salad Flatbread
with Artichokes, Garlic, Feta, and Olives

When you've got dough in the refrigerator, a hearty and filling vegetarian or vegan appetizer or main course is just minutes away. Baked at a high temperature, this flatbread has a thin, crispy crust and provides an alternative to a lettuce-based Greek salad with similar ingredients. If you like, serve this with fresh tomatoes or soup. If you use prepared pizza dough, sprinkle the crust with 2 teaspoons flaxseed before adding the toppings.

Serves 8 • Prep Time: 5 minutes • Cook Time: 15 minutes

Cornmeal, for sprinkling

1 pound Whole Wheat and **Flaxseed** Dough (page 116) or prepared pizza dough, preferably whole-grain, or a 10-inch prepared crust

Flour, for dusting

2 tablespoons **olive oil**

1 clove **garlic**, minced

9 ounces thawed frozen **artichoke** hearts, chopped, or 1½ cups drained canned **artichoke** hearts, chopped

¼ cup chopped pitted Kalamata or other ripe **olives**

4 ounces feta cheese, crumbled

1 teaspoon dried **oregano**

¼ cup coarsely chopped fresh Italian **parsley**, for garnish

1 Preheat the oven to 450°F. Place a broiler pan on the lower shelf of the oven and add 2 cups hot water. Sprinkle a rimmed baking sheet with cornmeal.

2 Place the dough on a floured surface, dust the top with flour, and roll or pat into a 12-inch oval. Transfer the dough to the prepared pan, then re-form it into an oval. In a small bowl, combine the olive oil and garlic. Brush half this mixture over the crust. Top the crust with the artichokes, then sprinkle with the olives, cheese, and oregano. Drizzle the remaining garlic oil over all.

3 Bake for 15 minutes or until both the edges of the crust and the cheese have browned. Transfer the flatbread to a cutting board and cut into pieces. Sprinkle each slice with Italian parsley and serve.

Calories 92 • Total Fat 7g • Saturated Fat 3g • Carbohydrates 5g • Protein 2g
Dietary Fiber 3g • Sodium 307mg

SLOW-SIMMERED TOMATO SAUCE
WITH RED WINE (PAGE 206)

WHOLE WHEAT AND
FLAXSEED BAGUETTES

Whole Wheat and Flaxseed Baguettes

We love these crusty baguettes at any meal: morning toast, sandwiches, or appetizers with dips or spreads. Adding water to the broiler pan placed on the lower shelf of the oven contributes to a crisp crust. An instant-read thermometer, inserted into the center of the loaf, is an easy way to tell if your bread is done.

Makes 2 loaves; serves 8 • Prep Time: 25 minutes • Cook Time: 25 to 27 minutes

¼ cup cornmeal, for sprinkling

2 pounds Whole Wheat and **Flaxseed** Dough (page 116)

All-purpose flour, for dusting

1. Sprinkle the cornmeal on a large rimmed baking sheet. Place the dough on a floured surface and dust very lightly with flour. Cut the dough in half with a serrated knife. Flour your hands. Working the dough as little as possible and adding flour as necessary, form one half into a 14-inch cylinder. Smooth the dough with your hands to form a soft, nonsticky skin. Pinch any seams together. Pinch each end into a point. Lightly flour any sticky places on the dough. The dough should feel soft and smooth all over, like a baby's skin, not at all sticky. Place the baguette on the prepared pan. Form the second loaf and place it on the pan.

2. Cover with a kitchen towel and let rest at room temperature for 40 minutes. (The dough will not rise, but will finish rising in the oven.)

3. Preheat the oven to 450°F. Carefully place a broiler pan on the lower shelf and add 2 cups hot water. Using a serrated knife, make five evenly spaced diagonal slashes, about 1 inch deep, across and down the length of each baguette, exposing the moist dough under the surface. Bake for 25 to 27 minutes, until the crust is a medium dark brown and an instant-read thermometer inserted into the center registers at least 190°F. Remove from the oven and transfer to a wire rack to cool.

Calories 70 • Total Fat 0.5g • Saturated Fat 0g • Carbohydrates 15g • Protein 2g
Dietary Fiber 1.5g • Sodium 220mg

I started going about my life—family, work, friends—with a few tweaks to manage my health.

~Roz Varon, television anchor/reporter

Whole Wheat and Flaxseed Boule

This versatile dough can be formed into different shapes, including the round loaf made here.

Makes 1 round loaf bread; serves 8 • Prep Time: 50 minutes • Cook Time: 35 minutes

2 pounds Whole Wheat and **Flaxseed** Dough (page 116)

All-purpose flour, for dusting

¼ cup cornmeal, for the baking sheet

1 To form into a loaf, transfer the dough to a floured surface and dust very lightly with flour. Flour your hands. Working the dough as little as possible and adding flour as necessary, form the dough into an 8-inch round. Lightly flour any sticky places on the dough. The dough should feel soft and smooth all over, like a baby's skin, not at all sticky. Pinch closed any seams and the ends. Sprinkle a large baking sheet with the cornmeal and transfer the dough to the prepared pan. Cover with a kitchen towel and let rest at room temperature for 40 minutes. (The dough will not rise very much; it will finish rising during baking.)

2 Preheat the oven to 450°F. Place the broiler pan on the lower rack of the oven and fill the pan with 2 cups hot water. Using a serrated knife, cut three 1-inch deep slashes across the top of the round loaf.

3 Bake the loaf for 35 minutes, or until an instant-read thermometer inserted into the center registers 190°F. Transfer the loaf to a wire rack to cool.

Calories 70 • Total Fat 0.5g • Saturated Fat 0g • Carbohydrates 15g
Protein 2g • Dietary Fiber 1.5g • Sodium 220mg

Flatbread with Grapes and Gruyère

A flatbread is a thinner, crispier dough that can be patted out to any shape, so that makes it easy on the cook. Although this sounds like an unusual flavor combination, the sweet grapes and salty, savory cheese make a delicious—and easy—combination. If you have the dough already made, all you do it pat it out, top with the ingredients, and bake. Take this flatbread when you're asked to bring an appetizer or something for a casual meal. Cave-aged Gruyère has the most flavor—nutty and savory—and is available at better grocery stores.

Serves 8 • Prep Time: 15 minutes
• Cook Time: 15 minutes

Cornmeal for sprinkling

1   pound Whole Wheat
    and **Flaxseed** Dough
    (page 116), prepared
    pizza dough, or ready
    to eat pizza crust

All-purpose flour,
for dusting

2   tablespoons **olive oil**

2   cups seedless **red
    grapes**, cut in half

4   ounces cave-aged
    Emmenthal or **Gruyère
    cheese**, shredded

1   Preheat the oven to 450°F. Sprinkle a baking sheet with cornmeal.

2   Place the dough on a floured surface, dust the top with flour, and roll or pat into a 12-inch oval. Transfer the dough to the prepared pan, then re-form it into an oval. Brush the olive oil over the crust. Top the crust with grapes, then sprinkle with the cheese.

3   Bake for 15 minutes, or until both the edges of the crust and the cheese have browned. Transfer the flatbread to a cutting board and cut into pieces.

Calories 123 • Total Fat 8g • Saturated Fat 3g • Carbohydrates 8.5g
Protein 4.5g • Dietary Fiber 0.5g • Sodium 49mg

Baja Bites

If you love fish, this dish includes lots of options to reel in some protein while preserving the flavor, fat-free. Fresh and fast, this south-of-the-border appetizer tastes wonderful as a dip with Baked Tortilla Chips (page 102), or warm corn or flour tortillas. Adapted from a recipe in *Eating Well Magazine*, this dish needs to be refrigerated for at least 20 minutes and up to 2 hours before serving, so the flavors blend. For a vegetarian or vegan alternative, use about 10 ounces of a vegetable protein, such as tofu, in place of the poached fish.

Serves 8 • Prep Time: 30 minutes • Cook Time: 6 minutes

1   pound white fish fillets, such as **halibut** or cod, cut into 2-inch pieces

1   to 2 small jalapeño **chiles**, seeded and finely chopped

½   teaspoon dried **oregano**

¼   teaspoon salt

½   large green **bell pepper**, seeded and slivered

½   large yellow or orange **bell pepper**, seeded and slivered

1   cup **Roasted Tomatoes and Garlic** (page 103) or canned tomatoes, drained

½   cup finely chopped **green onions**, with some green

¼   cup quartered pimiento-stuffed green **olives**

½   cup fresh lime juice (4 to 5 limes)

⅓   cup chopped fresh cilantro, plus more for garnish

1   small avocado, halved, pitted, peeled, and chopped

Warm corn or flour tortillas or baked corn chips, for serving

1   Place the fish in a large skillet and add water to cover. Bring to a boil over high heat. Remove from the heat, cover, and let poach for 6 minutes, or until the fish flakes when tested with a fork.

2   Transfer the poached fish to a large bowl with a slotted spoon. Add the chiles, oregano, salt, bell peppers, tomatoes, green onions, olives, lime juice, and cilantro. Toss to blend. Cover and refrigerate for at least 20 minutes.

3   When ready to serve, gently fold in the avocado and garnish with cilantro. Spoon the mixture into tortillas or use as a dip with corn chips.

Calories 294 • Total Fat 7g • Saturated Fat 1g • Carbohydrates 45g
Protein 17g • Dietary Fiber 7g • Sodium 243mg

The excuse for shopping we always wanted: health benefits!

It's the news clipping everyone needs from the December 2, 2005, *Wall Street Journal* article, "This Is Your Brain at the Mall: Why Shopping Makes You Feel So Good":

"When you are shopping to buy a gift or get something for yourself, either way it's kind of a treat," says Ms. Wazhma Samizay, who three years ago opened a Seattle boutique named Retail Therapy. "The concept of the store was about finding things that made people feel good."

According to the article, "Scientific research is now discovering what Samizay and many consumers have known all along: Shopping makes you feel good. A growing body of brain research suggests that shopping activates key areas of the brain, boosting our mood and making us feel better. Staring into a window display or discovering a hard-to-find toy appears to activate the brain's reward center, triggering the release of brain chemicals that give you a 'shopping high.'"

WOULD SOMEONE JUST TELL ME . . .

Q: When I get upset, I go back to my old habits of eating too many sweets to feel better. But I end up feeling worse. How can I stop this habit?

A: We understand. There is no quick fix, no magic pill to make this habit go away. The culture we live in sets us up to overeat and overuse food, while simultaneously telling us that we are never good enough the way we are.

It is a lot easier to tell someone to go on a diet than to help her figure out what emotions she has been burying for decades. If overusing food was a coping mechanism prior to breast cancer, it will be one post–breast cancer, unless she targets new strategies to solve the problem. See Recipe for Living Well "perfect storm" (page xxiii) for a list of problem solvers.

The news was bad.
I went to Bendel's.

Three doctors had already told me that the carat-size lump in my left breast was, in all likelihood, nothing to worry about. As a 37-year-old Chinese woman with no history of breast cancer in the family, my chances of a malignancy, they said, were lottery low. The radiologist who performed the routine biopsy last spring seemed less certain. She carried out the needle aspiration with brisk efficiency, extracting tissue samples via four staple-gun-like thrusts to the offending mass. After the fourth ka-chung, she flipped on the lights and turned to face me. "I'm not going to lie to you," she said. "It doesn't look great. I'd say your odds are about 50-50."

By Ellen J. Tien

Her honesty was cruelly refreshing. "I'll phone your regular doctor tomorrow with the lab results, and he'll call you," she said. "Good luck."

It occurred to me that when a doctor wishes you good luck, it might not be the world's best sign. I got dressed, walked out of the office, and did the only thing I really could do, under the circumstances. I went shopping.

F.A.O. Schwarz was conveniently situated on the corner, so I headed in and up, straight to the Star Wars section, where I gathered an armload of action figures for my 4-year-old son. That done, I went across the street to the Bergdorf Goodman men's store and chose a summer suit and a striped Etro shirt for my husband. The entire expedition took less than an hour.

Still, by the time I stepped out of Bergdorf, the city had changed. The unpredictable gold and gray sky of late spring had faded to black, hurling great canvases of rain over Midtown. Fifth Avenue was bouncing with raindrops, and not an available taxi was in sight. As I peered down the rows of cars, my arms laden with packages, I felt my first pang of despair.

Magically, an empty cab stopped directly in front of me. "You've got a whole lot of packages there," the driver said as I clambered in. I explained that they were gifts for my husband and son. "Lucky them," he said. "What's the occasion—did you just get a big new job?"

"Something like that," I said.

By noon the next day, the results were official. My new employer was invasive ductal carcinoma, and it was now my assignment to beat it. In the breath it took my doctor to say, "I have bad news: you have breast cancer," I was lifted into a whole

In shopping, there is an implicit future. When a salesperson assures you that the shearling coat you're buying will last forever, it helps you to believe that maybe you will, too.

different shopping arena. For the next few months, I walked the aisles of breast surgeons, oncologists, and radiation oncologists. I became versed in the brand names of chemotherapy treatments; I discovered a world where a single anti-nausea pill could cost $200. It was a grim and compelling sort of spree, the most high-stakes shopping imaginable.

Yet, oddly, I had never felt more sure-footed. I knew I had the skills. From the time I was old enough to point and say, "This one," it was clear I had been born with my mother's shopping genes. I bought my wedding dress in an hour, my apartment in a week. Now, I would sift through the shelves of medical terms and make order of them; I could remain unmoved by a flashy surgeon's sales pitch. Given the opportunity, I was more than ready to haggle with fate. In a way, I had been preparing for this moment all my life.

Shopping is a freighted activity—at once a task and a hobby, a necessity and a pleasure. The average American spends six hours a week shopping. Last winter, the Harvard Design School put retail in the canon with its 800-page *Guide to Shopping*. The Stanford Medical Center is conducting studies on the brain chemistry of compulsive shoppers. Like eating and gambling, shopping has managed to traverse the pale from pastime to illness.

In the face of serious physical illness, however, shopping takes on a different cast. Certainly, there is a deny-yourself-nothing mentality that flashes on in the psyche upon diagnosis (and then flashes right off, after you receive the first medical bill). Too, there's a desire to seek haven in a place where the inventory is guaranteed to be new and untainted by the blot of toxins or bad cells.

But more than an agent of acquisition, shopping can be an act of hope. The dying take stock of their possessions, the living add to them. Shopping implies that there are days ahead of you and good times to be had: a Christmas party that cries out for Cacharel's pink kimono-tied dress, a spring afternoon just right for Stephen Burrow's bright knits. In shopping, there is an implicit future. When a salesperson assures you that the shearling coat you're buying will last forever, it helps you to believe that maybe you will, too.

So, as I trudged through the stages of primary and adjuvant treatments—a Memorial Sloan-Kettering ID slotted neatly in my wallet behind my American Express card—I shopped. There was the peasant skirt I bought at Calypso after the first surgical consultation, the Ralph Lauren cable cashmere cardigans I bought after the third.

After a post-lumpectomy checkup, there were the clownishly oversize Adidas sneakers I picked

Much the same way we exulted over the words "grossly unremarkable" on the pathology reports of our tumors, we were buoyed by the normalcy of shopping. We browsed, not for the quick lozenge-effect of the latest fad, but for continuity. We ordered hairpieces that exactly matched our own hair. We bought makeup to simulate our precancer skin tones, blotches and all. No longer searching for a grail that could make us look taller or leaner, we shopped to look precisely the way we always had.

out for my son—a secret insurance policy that I would be around to see them fit. Even an 11th hour trip to the Dana-Farber Cancer Institute in Boston yielded four coveted Palio plates from a little shop on Newbury Street. When one surgeon suggested that I start a "cancer diary" to help me process the process, I stifled the urge to laugh in his face. Who needed a diary? I had my credit card statements.

Along the way, I encountered women in similar situations who were keeping retail chronicles of their own. A fashion designer told me how she ate lunch at Barneys before her chemotherapy sessions. A college professor recounted how she fought a brutal, chemically induced depression by trying on shoes. Every morning for six weeks, as I sat in the waiting room of Stich Radiation Center at New York-Presbyterian Hospital, I listened to women with cancer discussing and comparing their most recent purchases, be it lipstick, a wig, a bracelet, or a wheelchair.

Certainly, these women and I were only doing what women do every day: going to work, attending to our children, accruing details—and taking a quick spin around Saks somewhere in between. But for us, there was comfort in the routine. Much the same way we exulted over the words "grossly unremarkable" on the pathology reports of our tumors, we were buoyed by the normalcy of shopping. We browsed, not for the quick lozenge-effect of the latest fad, but for continuity. We ordered hairpieces that exactly matched our own hair. We bought makeup to simulate our precancer skin tones, blotches and all. No longer searching for a grail that could make us look taller or leaner, we shopped to look precisely the way we always had.

Last week, I had my final radiation session. To mark the occasion, I decided to walk from the hospital back to F.A.O. Schwarz. As I passed by store windows along the way, I was struck by the array of clothing, accessories, and beauty products that had been created in honor of Breast Cancer

In what had abruptly become a frighteningly circumscribed universe, shopping offered possibility, a forward stretch into seasons to come. Soothed by the familiar rhythms of a department store, I could distract myself from nausea and walk off waves of fatigue. Even on my shakiest days, I could convince myself that if I didn't find anything good on one floor, I would on the next. In shopping, as in all else, where there's hope, there's life.

Awareness Month: the T-shirts and tote bags, earrings and pink-laced sneakers.

Before my diagnosis, I thought of this October retail practice as slightly distasteful, the chic-ifying and merchandising of a serious disease. Now, there seemed to me a strange symmetry between these two worlds. Seen one way, breast cancer is not unlike Bendel's in that both are populated almost exclusively by women. Both create a sense of sorority. Both have a certain underpinning of secrecy. Just as some women hide their purchases from their husbands, other women hid their cancers from their employers and children, grandparents and coworkers.

While I have never been secretive about my spending habits, I did hide my cancer from all but my closest family and friends. I wanted to avoid the scrutiny that comes with illness, the conversations with information-hungry people who mask their curiosity as concern and use phrases like "we're rooting for you." I needed to minimize the crocodile tears, the gossip, the questions like "How can you go shopping at a time like this?"

How could I not? In what had abruptly become a frighteningly circumscribed universe, shopping offered possibility, a forward stretch into seasons to come. Soothed by the familiar rhythms of a department store, I could distract myself from nausea and walk off waves of fatigue. Even on my shakiest days, I could convince myself that if I didn't find anything good on one floor, I would on the next. In shopping, as in all else, where there's hope, there's life.

This thought-provoking column on retail therapy first appeared in the *New York Times*, October 20, 2002. It inspired community members in Kansas City, Missouri, to launch Back in the Swing Retail Therapy, the annual shopping experiential fundraiser, benefiting Back in the Swing USA.

Reprinted with permission of Ellen J. Tien and the *New York Times*.

Gratitude is one way to experience joy. It also brings us to the present. We cannot change the past, and worrying about the future is wasted energy. Gratitude for what we have now is a wonderful grounding practice and helps us spare ourselves from the wasted energy of regret and fear.

~Jane Murray, MD, Sastun Center of Integrative Health Care

CHAPTER FIVE
Salads and Side Dishes

Grateful

*"We can only be said to be alive in those moments when
our hearts are conscious of our treasures."*

~*Thornton Wilder*

Renowned positive psychology research pioneer Barbara Fredrickson, PhD,
has revealed that seeking joy, serenity, interest, hope, pride, amusement,
inspiration, awe, love, and gratitude are ways to "broaden and build" our
thinking in positive ways.

Joy in life is associated with the senses being alive . . . and being in tune
with the sights, sounds, and smells in your world. Get creative and discover
the possibilities of "broadening and building" your mind by combining flavors
that work just for you in each of these recipes. Own your taste buds! Omit
an ingredient, such as peanuts, if you have allergies or you'd rather substitute
almonds, for example. Although the given nutritional analysis will not still be
accurate, you will come up with a recipe that is right on target for you. Each of
these salads and side dishes are hearty and flavorful; they are easy to adapt to our
own tastes, which gives us practice in being mindful of our own uniqueness, as well.

Christie's Coleslaw

This coleslaw is worth driving to the famous central coast of California to savor. Since the 1990s, it's been a regular on the menu at Gayle's Bakery and Rosticceria in Capitola, where everything is made from scratch. The ginger and peanuts add a little twist that is just the right surprise.

Serves 6 • Prep Time: 10 minutes

1	small head (1½ pounds) red or **green cabbage**, or a mixture of both, shredded
6	**carrots**, grated
1	bunch **scallions**, thinly sliced (½ cup)
1	cup loosely packed cilantro leaves, coarsely chopped (from 1 bunch)
½	cup low-fat mayonnaise
2	tablespoons grated fresh **ginger**
2	tablespoons grated **onion**
⅓	cup sugar, or 2 tablespoons **honey**
½	cup rice vinegar
1	teaspoon salt
1	teaspoon pepper
¼	cup candied ginger, finely chopped
¼	cup peanuts, chopped

1 Combine the cabbage, carrots, scallions, and cilantro in a large bowl.

2 Whisk the mayonnaise, fresh ginger, onion, sweetener, rice vinegar, salt, and pepper together in a medium bowl until well mixed.

3 Toss the slaw with the dressing so that it is well coated.

4 Place the coleslaw in a serving dish and top with the candied ginger and the peanuts.

Calories 120 • Total Fat 5g • Saturated Fat 0.5g • Carbohydrates 13g
Protein 2g • Dietary Fiber 2.5g • Sodium 250 mg

Bodacious Broccoli Salad

Gayle Ortiz, the founder and owner of Gayle's Bakery and Rosticceria in Capitola, California, says, "This is one of our customers' favorite salads. It's tangy, rich with cheese, and crunchy with a bit of sweetness from the raisins. Give it a try, it's easy and super delicious." We wholeheartedly agree—it's amazingly addictive, with complementary flavors in every bite.

Serves 6-8, 1-cup servings • Prep Time: 10 minutes

½ cup (scant) mayonnaise

2 tablespoons **apple cider vinegar**

2 tablespoons sugar

¼ teaspoon salt

¼ teaspoon pepper

1 pound **broccoli**

¾ cup golden **raisins**

½ cup toasted **sunflower seeds**

1¼ cups grated sharp Cheddar cheese (5 ounces)

2 tablespoons grated **red onion**

1 Whisk together the mayonnaise, vinegar, sugar, salt, and pepper in a small bowl for the dressing and set aside.

2 Cut off 1 inch of the woody bottom of each broccoli stalk. Cut off the florets. Chop the florets into ½-inch pieces and grate the stems using the grater attachment of a food processor. You should have about 4 cups broccoli. Mix the broccoli, raisins, sunflower seeds, cheese, and onion in a large bowl. Pour the dressing over the salad and toss well.

Calories 198 • Total Fat 10g • Saturated Fat 1.5g • Carbohydrates 25g
Protein 4.5g • Dietary Fiber 5.5g • Sodium 598mg

Simple Quinoa

Leigh Wagner, MS, RD, LD, provided this side dish of protein that serves as a basic palette for your favorite vegetables—choose fresh for most nutrients, but frozen can be your best friend when you're home, hungry, and want to eat NOW!

Serves 4 • Prep Time: 15 minutes • Cook Time: 15 to 20 minutes

1 cup **quinoa**, rinsed and drained

¾ teaspoon sea salt

1¾ cups water

½ to ¾ cup chopped vegetables, such as **cabbage**, **carrots**, **broccoli**, **kale**, chard, **spinach**, **bell peppers**, or other favorites (optional)

2 cloves **garlic**, minced (optional)

¼ cup chopped **walnuts** or cashews (optional)

1 Place the quinoa, salt, and water in a medium saucepan. Bring to a boil, reduce the heat to low, cover, and let simmer for 15 to 20 minutes. Don't stir the grains while cooking.

2 During the last 5 to 7 minutes of cooking, toss in the chopped vegetables and/or minced garlic, if using, to steam over the top of the grains.

3 After the 15 to 20 minutes, test for doneness by tilting the pan to one side, making sure all of the water has been absorbed.

4 Toss in the nuts, if desired. Fluff with a fork and serve right away.

Calories 212 • Total Fat 7.5g • Saturated Fat 1g • Carbohydrates 30g
Protein 8g • Dietary Fiber 4g • Sodium 451mg

WHO KNEW?

Q: What is so good about quinoa?

A: Most commonly considered a grain, quinoa is actually a relative of leafy green vegetables, such as spinach, and is a rediscovered ancient "grain" once considered "the gold of the Incas." Not only is quinoa high in protein, the protein it supplies is *complete protein*, meaning that it includes all nine essential amino acids. So it is a great choice for vegans who are concerned about adequate protein intake. It is especially rich in the amino acid *lysine*, which is essential for tissue growth and repair. In addition to protein, quinoa features a host of other health-building nutrients. Because quinoa is a very good source of manganese, as well as a good source of magnesium, iron, copper, and phosphorus, this grain may be especially valuable for persons with migraine headaches, diabetes, and atherosclerosis.

PROFESSOR POSITIVE

Control: You're in charge, Marge!

Sometimes we all feel overwhelmed, as if our lives have spun out of control. When this happens to you, take a note from research that indicates having the perception that you have control is associated with better natural killer cells (i.e., the cancer-killing immune cells) function, versus not having the perception that you are in control. Of course, it is important to keep in mind that there *are* things in your life that you literally have no control over!

Studies of nursing home patients, reported in the August 1976 *Journal of Personality and Social Psychology,* demonstrated that allowing nursing home patients to exercise control over small tasks, such as taking care of a plant or choosing when to watch television, was enough to lengthen their lives by months, compared to their low-control counterparts.

So it is good advice to take control over some aspects of your life, even if in small ways, such as choosing a plant for your garden. Doing so will help you feel better, research says, and improve your overall health, as well.

Mexican Fruit Salad
with Honey-Lime Dressing

You can hear that little voice inside of you that says, "What can I have that will satisfy my sweet tooth and stay in the good-for-me category?" Whipping up this treat will satisfy that tooth and more—it's simply fruit in party clothes. This one is a fiesta of colors and flavors that will make you happy that you're being good to yourself. Use whatever fruit is in season (usually that's what's on sale) and vary the colors. This fruit salad will keep, covered, in the refrigerator for up to 3 days.

Serves 4 • Prep Time: 5 minutes

1   cup chopped fresh
    mango, papaya,
    or cantaloupe

1   cup fresh **blueberries**

1   cup chopped fresh
    honeydew melon or kiwi

1   cup fresh **pineapple**
    chunks

1   cup seedless **red grapes**
    or green grapes

1   tablespoon fresh
    orange zest

½   cup fresh **orange juice**

1   tablespoon fresh
    lemon juice

⅓   cup **honey**

¼   cup fresh lime juice

1   Combine the mango, blueberries, honeydew, pineapple, and grapes in a large bowl. Stir the orange zest, orange juice, and lemon juice in a small bowl, then pour over the fruit. Toss gently to blend. Cover and refrigerate until ready to serve.

2   Right before serving, whisk the honey and lime juice together in a small bowl. Pour over the salad, and toss to blend. Serve the salad in glass dishes.

Calories 218 • Total Fat 0.5g • Saturated Fat 0g • Carbohydrates 57g
Protein 2g • Dietary Fiber 4.5g • Sodium 6mg

New-Fashioned Spring Greens Salad

Here's the salad you've been waiting for all winter—just when strawberries come into season, create a vinaigrette dressing that will delight all of your senses and give you good reason to go green. In this recipe, adapted from the *Simply in Season* cookbook by Mary Beth Lind and Cathleen Hockman-Wert, simply use the ingredients that suit you at the moment.

Serves 4 • Prep Time: 15 minutes

8 cups mixed **greens**, such as green or red leaf lettuce, **spinach**, or **baby kale**

TOPPING OPTIONS

2 green **onions**, with some green, chopped

1 small **red onion**, cut into thin rings

1 cup bean sprouts or **radishes**

1 cup celery, chopped

2 cups sliced **mushrooms**

2 to 3 hard-boiled **eggs**, sliced

1 fresh **artichoke** (see page 139), thinly sliced

Chive blossoms, for color (optional)

STRAWBERRY VINAIGRETTE

1 cup **strawberries**

4 teaspoons rice vinegar

4 teaspoons fresh **lemon juice**

1 tablespoon pure **maple syrup**

¼ teaspoon salt

⅛ teaspoon garlic powder

⅛ teaspoon onion powder

⅛ teaspoon dried **basil** leaves

⅛ teaspoon dried parsley flakes

⅛ teaspoon pepper

¼ cup **olive oil**

1 For the salad, chop the mixed greens into bite-size pieces and place in a large bowl. Add your favorite topping options.

2 For the vinaigrette, puree the strawberries in a blender or food processor. Add the rice vinegar, lemon juice, maple syrup, salt, garlic powder, onion powder, dried basil, dried parsley, and pepper and blend until smooth. Gradually add the oil in a thin stream until the vinaigrette thickens.

3 Pour about ½ cup vinaigrette over the salad ingredients and toss to blend. The remaining vinaigrette can be refrigerated, covered, for up to 2 days.

Calories 259 • Total Fat 12g • Saturated Fat 3g • Carbohydrates 18g
Protein 10g • Dietary Fiber 6g • Sodium 274mg

I KNEW I WAS BACK IN THE SWING WHEN . . .

The area under my arm around my breast tissue finally got some mobility, years after my surgery. No one ever told me that it would be good to use massage therapy to keep the tissue from hardening. And now, through over a dozen sessions with my physical therapist, I finally, truly, feel like I'm back to normal. A word of caution: As this surgery site is near the breast/arm lymphatics, this kind of massage can be recommended or not, depending on your situation. Consult with your oncologist before receiving a massage.

~Pam Schlossman, RN

WHO KNEW?

Q: How do I prepare a fresh artichoke for a salad?

A: Thanks to Leigh Wagner, MS, LD, RD, of the University of Kansas Integrative Medicine Center, and Chef Cody Hogan, of Lidia's in Kansas City, for these easy tips:

1   Handle one artichoke at a time, and handle carefully to avoid pricking yourself on the sharp tops of the leaves.

2   Stir the juice of 1 lemon (about 3 tablespoons) into 1 quart water. This is called *acidulated water*.

3   Trim and/or pull off the thick, outside leaves, and leave the tender, yellowish center. Cut off the bottom of the stem leaving about 1 inch. Using a vegetable peeler or paring knife, peel the stem. Cut across the top of the artichoke to remove the pointed tops of the leaves. Using a teaspoon, remove the choke from the center of the artichoke until scraped clean.

4   Place in acidulated water until all the artichokes are prepared in this manner.

5   To prepare for the salad, remove one artichoke at a time. Starting at the stem, slice thinly (about ⅛ inch) and add to the salad.

Optimism protects your heart.

As Jimmie C. Holland, MD, and Sheldon Lewis wrote in their book *The Human Side of Cancer*, there is overwhelming proof showing that "how you cope with your illness can improve your overall quality of life."

A March 2011 study in *Archives of Internal Medicine* suggests a mind-body connection in the recovery from coronary disease. The study reports that heart patients with more positive attitudes about their recovery had about a 30 percent greater chance of survival after fifteen years than patients with pessimistic attitudes.

This is the longest, largest study to track survival, according to lead author John Barefoot, professor emeritus at Duke University Medical Center in Durham, North Carolina.

"Our research shows better physical recovery and a higher likelihood of survival is linked to attitude—personal beliefs about their illness," Barefoot says.

The scientists followed the patients for approximately fifteen years. Even after controlling for a range of factors—including the severity of their coronary disease, age, gender, income, and depression—a good attitude about recovery still correlated with better health years later.

On why a more positive outlook is better for long-term health, Barefoot has two hypotheses:

> *People with positive expectations are better at coping with their illness, so they will be better able to focus on their coping process and solve problems. They're less likely to give up. They'll try to solve the problems rather than just worry about them. Also, people with positive expectations may have less of a stress reaction physiologically than people with stress.*

Fresh Orange, Red Onion, and Pomegranate Salad

When pomegranates are in season in late fall and through the winter, cut one in half, then scoop out the seeds (arils) for this dish—or just to snack on. According to the Beller Nutritional Institute (Bellernutritionalinstitute.com), pomegranate seeds make an excellent choice for daily snacks and can work into almost anybody's healthy resolutions. Not only are they rich in fiber, recent research has also shown that the oil in the seeds have powerful antioxidants that may aid in preventing cancer development. Chew the seeds thoroughly to release their potent oil—your immune system will thank you. For more information, check out the graphic way to release the seeds at Pomegranates.org/nomess. html. This salad makes you feel great just to look at it, and even better when you eat it. A teaspoon of Work of Art Drizzle on each salad works even more magic with garlic, olive oil, and lemon. Serve this over baby spinach, mixed greens, or curly endive, if you like.

Serves 4 • Prep Time: 15 minutes

4 medium **oranges**

2 cups **fresh greens**, such as baby **spinach**

¼ cup thinly sliced **red onion**, cut into slivers

4 teaspoons Work of Art Drizzle (page 145)

1 cup fresh **pomegranate seeds** (arils)

1 Cut off the ends of each orange with a sharp knife. Then cut off the rest of the orange rind and as much of the white pith as possible. Cut each orange horizontally into 1-inch slices.

2 Arrange the greens on four plates. Alternate the orange slices with red onion on top of the greens.

3 Spoon a teaspoon of the drizzle over the orange mixture. Top each salad with ¼ cup pomegranate seeds and serve.

Calories 105 • Total Fat 0.5g • Saturated Fat 0g • Carbohydrates 25g
Protein 2.5g • Dietary Fiber 5g • Sodium 14mg

Awe and wonder help us feel that there
is more than just us in the universe—

Wilted Greens with Warm Cranberry Vinaigrette

Usually a wilted salad has a hot bacon dressing, but this cranberry burst of flavor can more than make up for the bacon. For another meal, cover and chill leftover vinaigrette to enjoy over a green salad that could also include chicken, turkey, or other meat . . . or a meatless protein, such as tofu. Look for a robustly colored mix of baby greens that includes baby chard and beet greens for the best color, karma-for-your-core, and flavor.

Serves 4 • Prep Time: 5 minutes

1¼ cups Warm Cranberry Vinaigrette (recipe follows)

4 cups sturdy **baby greens**, such as **spinach**, **chard**, **beet greens**, and **kale**

1 Heat the vinaigrette in a saucepan over medium-high heat until hot, but not boiling. Remove from the heat.

2 Arrange 1 cup baby greens on each plate and spoon about 5 tablespoons or roughly ¼ cup vinaigrette over the greens. Serve immediately.

Calories 7 • Total Fat 0g • Saturated Fat 0g • Carbohydrates 1g • Protein 1g Dietary Fiber 0.5g • Sodium 24 mg

*and that our problems pale in comparison
to the grandeur of nature.*

~Jane Murray, MD, Sastun Center of Integrative Health Care

Warm Cranberry Vinaigrette

We like recipes that can do double, triple, and quadruple duty, and this is a great example. When cranberries are in season, grab lots of bags and throw them in your freezer so you can make this vinaigrette and drizzling sauce whenever you want. Serve this warm as a sauce over Thanksgiving turkey, chicken breasts, or a veggie burger. Enjoy it over wilted greens. You can also cover and chill leftover vinaigrette to enjoy at lunch over a fresh green salad that includes a lean protein. This vinaigrette is adapted from a recipe by cookbook author Karen Adler.

Makes about 2½ cups; serves 8 • Prep Time: 5 minutes • Cook Time: 5 to 7 minutes

1   cup **cranberries**

⅓   cup **agave nectar**

¼   cup **apple cider vinegar**

¼   cup plus 2 tablespoons **orange juice**

2   tablespoons **olive oil**

1   teaspoon Dijon mustard

½   teaspoon **red pepper flakes**

½   teaspoon ground **cinnamon**

½   teaspoon garlic salt

1   In a medium saucepan, heat the cranberries, agave nectar, and vinegar over medium-high heat, stirring, for 5 to 7 minutes, until the cranberries pop. Remove from the heat and stir in the orange juice, olive oil, mustard, red pepper flakes, cinnamon, and garlic salt until well blended. Enjoy warm or at room temperature. The dressing will keep, covered, in the refrigerator for up to 2 weeks.

Calories 90 • Total Fat 3.5g • Saturated Fat 0.5g
Carbohydrates 13g • Protein 0g • Dietary Fiber 0.5g • Sodium 75mg

Citrus Sesame Chicken Salad

Try chicken, shrimp, or toasted tofu in this wonderful dish: The dressing's really the thing. The flavor comes from the intriguing combination of orange and sesame. Bring this on a platter to a gathering or a friend, and watch it disappear. Toasted sesame oil (it has a medium brown color) can be found in the Asian section of the grocery store.

Serves 4 ½-cup servings • Prep Time: 15 minutes

CITRUS VINAIGRETTE

2   teaspoons toasted **sesame oil**

½   teaspoon grated **orange zest** or orange extract

¼   cup plus 2 tablespoons fresh **orange juice**

     Salt and pepper

2   cups chopped romaine

2   cups diced cooked **chicken**, **shrimp**, **halibut**, or **vegetable protein**

1   cup chopped fresh **orange**, or drained and rinsed canned mandarin **oranges**

½   cup chopped **green onions**, with some green

1   teaspoon toasted **sesame seeds**, for garnish

1   For the vinaigrette, whisk the sesame oil, orange zest, and orange juice in a bowl. Season to taste with salt and pepper.

2   Arrange the greens on a platter and top with the chicken, orange, and green onions. Cover and chill for up to 4 hours before serving. Then drizzle with the vinaigrette and sprinkle with sesame seeds to serve.

Calories 109 calories • Total Fat 3g • Saturated Fat 0.3g • Carbohydrates 8g Protein 0g • Dietary Fiber 1.5g • Sodium 133mg

WHO KNEW?

Q: How do I toast sesame seeds?

A: It's easy and the aroma is amazing. Here's how: For stovetop toasting, use a wide frying pan. Heat the sesame seeds on medium heat, shaking the pan occasionally, for about 3 minutes. Remove the pan from the heat when the seeds start to darken and become fragrant. For oven toasting, preheat the oven to 325°F. Spread the seeds out on a rimmed baking sheet. Bake for about 15 minutes, until the seeds start to brown and become fragrant. For both methods, allow the toasted seeds to cool before using in a recipe. Store in a covered jar at room temperature.

I didn't wake up every morning or go to sleep each night with the word "cancer" circling in my head.

~Anonymous

Work of Art Drizzle

Here's the back story of this recipe: Legend has it that a woman working in a Greek taverna traded the secret ingredients in this special vinaigrette to the owner of the restaurant, in exchange for a painting that hung over the bar. Well worth it! Just a 20-calorie teaspoon of this dressing does wonders on salads, vegetables, fish, or chicken. Leftover dressing will keep, covered, at room temperature for 2 to 3 days but tastes best freshly made.

Makes ¼ cup (12 teaspoons); serves 12 • Prep Time: 5 minutes

1 large clove **garlic**, minced

1 teaspoon kosher salt

3 tablespoons extra-virgin **olive oil**

1 tablespoon fresh **lemon juice**

1 In a small bowl, mash the garlic and salt together with a fork until you have a paste. Stir in the olive oil until the garlic blends into the oil, then stir in the lemon juice.

TO USE this vinaigrette for a dish with 30 percent fat, serve it with at least 12 ounces lean protein, such as boneless, skinless chicken breast; turkey; tofu; or 6 ounces of lean protein plus 2 cups cooked Power Pilaf (page 221), rice, or pasta.

Calories 20 • Total Fat 2g • Saturated Fat 0g • Carbohydrates 0g • Protein 0g Dietary Fiber 0g • Sodium 200mg

WHO KNEW?

Q: Should all my fruits and vegetables be organic?

A: It is important to note that there has not been, to date, a randomized clinical trial that has demonstrated that organic foods are better for your health. That having been said, it is also important to point out that these foods are produced without potentially harmful, environmentally long-lasting agricultural chemicals that have been commonly used on conventional food products since the 1950s. The label requirements and research makes this an ever-changing field.

For the most up-to-date information on what qualifies and what's new, check out:

WHOLE FOODS MARKET: WholeFoods.com

ORGANIC TRADE ASSOCIATION: ota.com

ORGANIC FARMING RESEARCH ASSOCIATION: ofrf.org

USDA'S NATIONAL ORGANIC PROGRAM: ams.usda.gov/nop/

PROFESSOR POSITIVE
Do something nice for someone else.

Sometimes when we are feeling depressed and going through a stressful period, the last thing that you think you can do is help someone else. Interestingly, helping someone else is one of the best ways to improve your happiness! Find an organization to volunteer at that you are passionate about: Walk a dog at an animal shelter; build a home with Habitat for Humanity; volunteer at a retirement center, or tutor children having trouble at school, for example. You will be amazed at how much better you and the person or animal you are helping feel as a result, notes the book *Altruism and Health*, edited by Stephen Post.

Orange and Apricot Salad over Fresh Greens

If a salad could be called a friend, this is your best buddy. It is an intriguing mix of sweet and savory, with just a hint of cinnamon in the no-fat dressing. Orange zest is simply the rind of an orange; the orange oils in the grated zest help give this salad its wonderful flavor.

Serves 4 • Prep Time: 5 minutes

½ cup dried apricots, soaked in boiling water for 30 minutes and drained

1 (15-ounce) can mandarin **oranges**, drained and rinsed

1 teaspoon freshly grated **orange zest**

2 tablespoons **orange juice**

2 tablespoons **honey**, **agave nectar**, or **sorghum**

2 tablespoons fresh **lemon juice**

½ teaspoon ground **cinnamon**

2 cups shredded romaine

2 cups baby **spinach**

¼ cup toasted **walnuts**, chopped

1 Chop the apricots into bite-size pieces and combine with the mandarin oranges in a bowl. In a small bowl, whisk the orange zest, orange juice, sweetener, lemon juice, and cinnamon until well blended. Combine the dressing with the fruit.

2 To serve, arrange the romaine and spinach on four plates. Top each plate with one-fourth of the fruit mixture and garnish with one-fourth of the walnuts.

Calories 189 • Total Fat 5g • Saturated Fat 0.5g • Carbohydrates 37g Protein 3g • Dietary Fiber 4.5g • Sodium 18mg

Somewhere Over the Rainbow Slaw

Everyone from Auntie Em to Dorothy will love this lightened-up treat. One bite, click your heels three times, and off to Oz you go. After making this yourself, you'll say, "There's no place like home!"

Serves 4 • Prep Time: 10 minutes

½ cup finely chopped **red bell pepper**

½ cup finely chopped **napa**, **savoy**, or bagged shredded **cabbage**, washed and dried

½ cup shredded **carrot**

½ cup finely chopped **green onion**, with some green

2 tablespoons finely chopped fresh Italian **parsley**

2 teaspoons minced **shallots**

2 tablespoons prepared **horseradish**

1 small clove **garlic**, minced

3 tablespoons fresh **lemon juice**

2 tablespoons water

1 teaspoon Dijon mustard

Salt and pepper

1 For the slaw, combine the bell pepper, cabbage, carrot, green onion, and parsley in a medium bowl.

2 For the dressing, combine the shallots, horseradish, garlic, lemon juice, water, and mustard in a small bowl. Whisk, then season with salt and pepper.

3 When ready to serve, pour the dressing over the slaw and toss to blend. Serve on four plates.

Calories 29 • Total Fat 0.5g • Saturated Fat 0g • Carbohydrates 6g Protein 1g • Dietary Fiber 1.5g • Sodium 70mg

As time went by after my treatment ended, I actually had to remind myself that I even had cancer. Friends would talk about cancer survivors, and I would not immediately identify with that group.

~*Elaine Nelson, elementary school teacher*

WHO KNEW?

Q: Why is everyone telling me to eat cabbage?

A: The Beller Nutritional Institute (Bellernutritionalinstitute.com) reports that cruciferous vegetables, such as cabbage, may be one of your strongest nutritional tools and are being studied extensively. Research with humans has suggested that cruciferous vegetables can alter estrogen metabolism in your body so that you are left with less of the stronger estrogens and more of the weaker ones. Health experts believe that having a lower level of the stronger estrogens may help reduce the risk of cancer recurrence in some women.

According to Rachel Beller, "Aim for having at least one serving of cruciferous vegetables daily. That's only half a cup cooked. When it comes to cruciferous vegetables, a little bit can go a long way."

Some familiar cruciferous vegetables are:

Cabbage	Cauliflower	Bok choy
Swiss chard	Horseradish	Arugula
Mustard greens	Brussels sprouts	Kale
Turnip greens	Collard greens	Rutabagas
Turnips	Radishes	Kohlrabi
Watercress	Broccoli	

Parisian Raspberry and Blue Cheese Salad

All we can say is "Yum!" Inspired by a trip to Paris, this dish is easy to pull together and fabulous enough to serve for a girlfriends' lunch. If you're not a blue cheese fan, swap out for feta. The dressing also includes olive oil and lemon juice.

Serves 4 • Prep Time: 10 minutes

4 cups baby **spinach**

4 cooked boneless, skinless **chicken breasts**, **Gardein**, or firm **tofu**, thinly sliced

2 cups fresh **raspberries**

1 cup **Raspberry** Vinaigrette (recipe follows)

¼ cup crumbled blue cheese or feta cheese, or toasted **walnuts**

1 Arrange the spinach on four large plates. Top with chicken and scatter with raspberries. Drizzle with the vinaigrette, then top with cheese and serve.

Calories 212 • Total Fat 6g • Saturated Fat 2.5g • Carbohydrates 9g
Protein 29.5g • Dietary Fiber 4.5g • Sodium 195mg

PROFESSOR POSITIVE

It's Friday, and I'm in love!

Oxytocin, sometimes called the "love hormone," is a hormone in our body that responds to touch, hugging, and close interpersonal contact. Not only does this hormone help create pair bonds in mammals (connecting mother to child and partners to each other) it also has the ability to reduce damaging and immune system—suppressing stress hormones, as reported in the February 29, 2000 *Psychological Review*. Next time stress is getting you down, ask your partner for a hug, seek out a friend, or go out and get a relaxing massage. Fight that stress the oxytocin love-hormone way.

Raspberry Vinaigrette

Drizzle this perky, raspberry-colored vinaigrette over salad, chicken, fish, bean- or vegetable-based protein, or raw vegetables, for a taste you might savor in a Parisian bistro.

Makes 1 cup; serves 4 • Prep Time: 5 minutes

1   cup fresh or thawed frozen **raspberries**

2   tablespoons finely chopped **shallots**

3   tablespoons vegetable or chicken broth

3   tablespoons **red wine** or raspberry vinegar

2   tablespoons **honey**

1   tablespoon Dijon mustard

1   clove **garlic**, minced

2   tablespoons **olive oil**

    Salt and pepper

1   Combine the raspberries, shallots, broth, vinegar, honey, mustard, garlic, and olive oil in a food processor or blender and puree.

2   Pour the mixture through a fine-mesh strainer into a bowl to remove the seeds; discard the solids in the sieve. Season with salt and pepper.

3   Use right away or transfer to a glass jar with a lid. This keeps, covered, in the refrigerator for about 5 days. Simply shake to blend.

Calories 30 • Total Fat 2g • Saturated Fat 10g • Carbohydrates 3g
Protein 0g • Dietary Fiber 0.5g • Sodium 35mg

Aromatase Inhibitors and Heart Health

In December 2008, the U.S. Food and Drug Administration added a warning label to anastrozole, an aromatase inhibitor marketed as Arimidex, citing a potential increased risk for heart disease. Aromatase inhibitors, which also include Femara and Aromasin, prevent the production of estrogen, which some cancers need to grow and spread. (Tamoxifen, another drug frequently prescribed for breast cancer patients with estrogen-sensitive tumors, blocks the effect of estrogen in breast tissue.) Under current guidelines, the two drugs may be used in either order for the several years of treatment typically recommended.

"Overall, there is a 26% increased risk in heart events—heart attack, angina and heart failure—for women taking aromatase inhibitors for longer duration," which typically means more than three years, says the lead author of the study, Dr. Eitan Amir (Princess Margaret Hospital, Toronto, Ontario), at a press conference at the 2010 Annual San Antonio Breast Cancer Symposium (SABCS), where the new study was presented.

"But those are relative statistics, and they can be a bit misleading," according to Dr. Amir. "A relative risk compares the risk in two different groups of people. Another measure—absolute risk—refers to one person's actual risk of developing the disease over a given time period. In this study, the absolute risk to any one woman taking an aromatase inhibitor was less alarming. Only 1% more got heart disease," Dr. Amir says. But the risk among those who already had risk factors for heart disease, such as high blood pressure, was as high as 7 percent. "Aromatase inhibitors are being given routinely to many [breast cancer] patients," says Dr. Amir. And not everyone gets the same benefit, he added, so treatment should be based not just on breast cancer risk, but on the patient's cardiovascular profile and other health risks. "

According to Jennifer Klemp, PhD, MPH, one reason that this may be happening is "because estrogen plays a favorable role on the lipids; without estrogen production, an imbalance (elevated LDL) occurs that is more frequently seen in women on aromatase inhibitors."

One option would be to switch from one drug to the other, to avoid staying on aromatase inhibitors long-term, Dr. Amir says. When he compared women who used aromatase inhibitors first to those who used tamoxifen first, the risk for serious adverse effects was similar. But there was a hint that switching drugs reduced the risk of death from other causes.

According to Klemp, "This is a cost/benefit ratio that needs to be discussed with the patient by the provider."

Still, the findings, although preliminary, are no surprise to Julie R. Gralow, MD, director of breast medical oncology at Seattle Cancer Care Alliance, who reviewed the study results but was not involved in it. As with much of medical practice, decisions must be made on a case-by-case basis, Dr. Gralow noted.

Asian Chicken Salad
with Fresh Ginger Vinaigrette

One. Two. Three. Four. And you've got lunch for a day at the office—or a long drive with only fast food available along the highway. First, whip up this fabulous vinaigrette and keep the extra in the refrigerator; second, open a bag of broccoli slaw; third, add some cooked chicken or firm tofu; fourth, drizzle with the dressing. Unlike other salads, the broccoli slaw will stand up to the dressing, so you can mix it all together and then take it with you. Keep chilled in an insulated lunch cooler. Yum! The Fresh Ginger Vinaigrette also includes shallots, soy, and garlic.

Serves 4 • Prep Time: 5 minutes

2   cups cubed or shredded cooked **chicken** or **tofu**

12 ounces bagged **broccoli** slaw

½   cup Fresh **Ginger** Vinaigrette (recipe follows)

1   Place the chicken and broccoli slaw in a bowl. Toss with the vinaigrette. Serve right away, or cover and chill until serving.

Calories 146 • Total Fat 3.5g • Saturated Fat 1g • Carbohydrates 5.5g Protein 23g • Dietary Fiber 2g • Sodium 80mg

WOULD SOMEONE JUST TELL ME . . .

Q: What kind of self-talk can I use to have fun and enjoy my life, even when I have a scan that day or in the next week? I get so fearful and worried and upset for the whole week.

A: We understand. It is normal to dread scans, be fearful, and ask "What if?" questions. Try to reframe your thinking this way. Say to yourself, "I am part of my medical team. Before I start asking myself 'What if?' questions, I need results, just like my health care practitioners, prior to interpreting next steps. Worrying and overanalyzing are self-defeating and will not be helpful."

Fresh Ginger Vinaigrette

With a whopping 3 tablespoons of freshly grated ginger, this recipe packs a load of flavor. It is a versatile marinade or dressing for greens, squash, asparagus, beans, broccoli, tomatoes, and just about whatever you grow in your garden. Toss it with poultry, pork, seafood, and other lean proteins, too. To use this vinaigrette for a dish with 30 percent fat, serve it with 6 ounces of lean protein plus 2 cups cooked Power Pilaf (page 221), rice, or pasta.

Makes 1 cup; serves 8 • Prep Time: 5 minutes

3   tablespoons vegetable broth

3   tablespoons fresh lime juice

3   tablespoons grated fresh **ginger**

2   tablespoons finely chopped **shallots**

1   tablespoon **honey**

1   tablespoon **soy sauce**

1   clove **garlic**, minced

2   tablespoons **olive oil**

1   Combine the broth, lime juice, ginger, shallots, honey, soy sauce, garlic, and olive oil in a glass jar with a lid. Secure the lid and shake to blend. This keeps, covered, in the refrigerator for about 5 days.

Calories 20 • Total Fat 2g • Saturated Fat 0g • Carbohydrates 2.5g
Protein 0g • Dietary Fiber 0g • Sodium 50mg

Mediterranean Tuna Salad with Roasted Red Peppers

Gloppy tuna salad gets a fresh-tasting makeover in this easy recipe. Take this with you on a busy day, or arrange the peppers on a white platter, top with the tuna mixture and parsley, and take to a potluck occasion as a salad or appetizer. Be prepared for second servings and to give out the recipe. Instead of tuna, you can lightly beat 2 large eggs or equivalent egg substitute and stir them into the pilaf during the last minute of cooking until the shreds of egg are fully cooked (as you would do for fried rice). Add 1 tablespoon olive oil in place of the oil from the tuna and mix in the remaining ingredients.

Note: Piquillo (little beak) peppers from northern Spain are well worth seeking out for this recipe. Costco or better grocery stores will have them packed in jars. These small, conical peppers are roasted over embers, which gives them a distinct sweet, spicy, slightly smoky flavor. Unlike bell peppers, they aren't good raw but are delicious when roasted, peeled, and deseeded. Piquillo peppers stuffed with tuna is a dish you'll see in tapas or little plates restaurants.

Serves 4 • Prep Time: 10 minutes • Cook Time: 15 minutes

1	cup water
1¼	cups uncooked Power Pilaf mix (page 221)
1	(6 ½-ounce) can **tuna** packed in **olive oil**
	Grated zest and juice of 1 **lemon**
1	clove **garlic**, minced
½	teaspoon dried **oregano**
4	jarred roasted **red pepper** halves, or 8 jarred whole roasted **piquillo peppers**, cut into large strips
¼	cup chopped fresh Italian **parsley**

1 Bring the water to a boil in a saucepan over medium-high heat. Add the pilaf mix and cook, covered, for 10 minutes or until tender. Drain off any water and fluff with a fork.

2 Add the tuna with its oil, the lemon zest and juice, garlic, and oregano. Stir to blend, breaking up the tuna. Arrange the strips of pepper on a serving platter, mound the tuna salad on top, and sprinkle with parsley.

Calories 131 • Total Fat 4g • Saturated Fat 0.5g • Carbohydrates 7.5g Protein 15g • Dietary Fiber 2.5g • Sodium 170mg

Wild Rice and Cranberry Harvest Salad

This salad has all of the sweetness of a carrot cake, with a little zip from the onions as well. Perhaps it's too big a leap to think of this with a candle in it on that special occasion, so try making this as a "bring a dish" item to Thanksgiving. When you take this one, we predict that you'll be welcomed with open arms, then asked for the recipe before the meal's end. And to make it easy on you, too, you can make this a day ahead. You can also prepare and freeze wild rice ahead of time; it keeps in the freezer for about 3 months.

Serves 12 • Prep Time: 15 minutes • Cook Time: 45 minutes

1 cup water

1 cup **vegetable broth** or chicken broth

1 cup **wild rice**

1 cup dried **cranberries**

1 cup golden **raisins**

1 cup chopped **green onions**, with some green

5 tablespoons **pine nuts**, toasted

½ cup chopped fresh Italian **parsley**

FRESH ORANGE DRESSING

2 tablespoons grated **orange zest**

½ cup fresh **orange juice**

¼ cup **apple cider vinegar**

¼ cup **olive oil**

Salt and pepper

1 Bring the water and broth to a boil. Add the rice and bring to a boil. Reduce the heat, cover, and simmer, stirring occasionally, for about 40 minutes, until tender, but still slightly firm to the bite.

2 Drain the rice and transfer it to a large bowl and let cool. Stir the cranberries, raisins, green onions, pine nuts, and parsley into the rice.

3 For the dressing, whisk the orange zest, orange juice, and vinegar in a small bowl. Gradually whisk in the olive oil. Season to taste.

4 Add enough dressing to the wild rice salad to coat as you toss and blend. Cover and chill the salad for up to 24 hours before serving.

Calories 199 • Total Fat 7.5g • Saturated Fat 0.6g • Carbohydrates 32g
Protein 4g • Dietary Fiber 2.5g • Sodium 253mg

Take a deep breath, stretch, and become immersed in yoga.

According to researcher Karen Mustia, PhD, MPH, of the University of Rochester Medical Center, and her colleagues, doing yoga, in addition to chemotherapy, regularly for four weeks improves sleep quality, reduces dependency on sedative medication, reduces fatigue, and improves overall quality of life. Their research was presented at the June 2010 annual meeting of the American Society of Clinical Oncology.

MINDFUL PRACTICES USED TO PROMOTE OVERALL HEALTH

Jane Murray, MD, integrative medicine specialist, suggests that we consider the mind-body practices that focus on the interactions among the brain, mind, body, and behavior, with the intent to use the mind to affect physical functioning and promote health. Examples of mind-body practices include deep-breathing exercises, guided imagery, hypnotherapy, progressive muscle relaxation, *qi gong* (an ancient Chinese healing martial art), yoga and tai chi, a slow set of movements and focused breathing techniques intended to improve blood flow and movement of *qi* for health and internal balance.

MAKING YOGA FIT YOU

Research is ongoing on yoga as a mind-body practice that benefits breast cancer survivors. The various styles of yoga used for health purposes typically combine physical postures, breathing techniques, and meditation or relaxation. People use yoga as part of a general health regimen and also for a variety of health conditions. Use caution, however, in beginning a yoga regimen, to ensure that the physical requirements fit your practice.

Seafood Salad Louis

Adapted from a *Better Homes & Gardens* recipe, this version has a lot going for it—fresh and updated flavor, lots of crunch, and easy preparation. Serve retro-style, in a glass bowl surrounded by tomato and lemon wedges; in hollowed-out garden tomatoes; or mounded on a bed of sliced tomatoes and lemons on a platter. If you like, substitute a vegetable protein for the halibut and shrimp. The hearty vegetables help this salad to stay fresh and delicious for a day or two, kept covered in the refrigerator.

Serves 8 • Prep Time: 15 minutes

½ cup low-fat cottage cheese or ricotta cheese

2 tablespoons skim **milk**, or more as needed

1 tablespoon **tomato** paste

2 tablespoons finely diced jarred roasted **red pepper**

2 tablespoons thinly sliced **green onion**, with some green

Salt and pepper

2 cups shredded romaine

1 cup shredded red **cabbage**

½ cup shredded **carrot**

6 ounces **halibut**, **flounder**, or **cod** fillet, steamed until it flakes easily with a fork, cut into bite-size pieces

6 ounces peeled and cooked **shrimp**

Tomatoes, cut into wedges or sliced, for garnish

Lemons, cut into wedges or sliced, for garnish

1 For the dressing, combine the cheese, skim milk, and tomato paste in a food processor or blender and process until smooth. Transfer to a bowl and stir in the red pepper and green onion. Add more skim milk, if necessary, to make a mayonnaise-like consistency. Season to taste. Cover and chill until ready to serve.

2 In a large bowl, combine the romaine, red cabbage, carrot, fish, and shrimp and gently toss. Spoon the dressing over the salad and gently toss to blend. Keep covered and chilled until ready to serve. Garnish with tomatoes and lemons.

Calories 35 • Total Fat 1g • Saturated Fat 0.3g • Carbohydrates 3g
Protein 4g • Dietary Fiber 0.3g • Sodium 153mg

Roasted Apples and Squash with Rosemary

If you've never thought about an apple as a fruit to roast, this will have new appeal. One taste and you will have discovered a new way to get your apple a day. As a side dish for a holiday or celebratory dinner, this one has it all—fragrant aroma, delicious flavor, and ease of preparation. Serve this with the holiday turkey, or a turkey- or soy-based sausage. You can find butternut squash already cubed, fresh or frozen, or buy a squash and peel, seed, and cube your own.

Serves 8 • Prep Time: 10 minutes • Cook Time: 30 minutes

1   medium **onion**, coarsely chopped

2   Granny Smith **apples**, peeled, cored, and cubed

1   pound cubed **butternut squash**

1   tablespoon chopped fresh **rosemary**

3   cups vegetable broth

    Salt and pepper

    Fresh **rosemary** sprigs and thin-sliced Granny Smith **apple**, for garnish

1   Preheat the oven to 425°F. Combine the onion, apples, squash, and rosemary in a large baking dish. Pour in the broth and stir to moisten. Roast for 30 minutes, stirring halfway through, or until the butternut squash is tender when pierced with a fork.

2   Season to taste. Garnish with rosemary sprigs and sliced apple.

Calories 49 • Total Fat 0g • Saturated Fat 0g • Carbohydrates 13g
Protein 0.5g • Dietary Fiber 1.5g • Sodium 355mg

I settled with the thoughts of metastatic cancer as a chronic illness.

~Donna Pelletier, cancer survivorship advocate

Orange-Glazed Carrots with Fresh Mint

You've always heard that carrots are good for your eyes—now we give you a beautiful way to serve them that is a visual feast, inside and out. Look for bunches of young and slender carrots with the green tops for this recipe, perfect for a special cool weather dinner in spring or fall. Simply arrange the roasted carrots on a white platter and sprinkle with chopped mint. They're delicious warm, cold, or at room temperature.

Serves 8 • Prep Time: 10 minutes • Cook Time: 25 minutes

4   bunches fresh **carrots** with green tops (about 32), trimmed with some of the green still showing

1   tablespoon **olive oil**

    Salt

1   tablespoon **honey**

    Grated zest and juice of 2 **oranges** or blood oranges

2   tablespoons chopped fresh mint, for garnish

1   Preheat the oven to 375°F. Scrub the carrots with a vegetable brush under cool, running water. Pat dry and arrange on a large rimmed baking sheet. Brush the carrots with oil and season with salt.

2   Roast for 15 minutes, until almost tender or done to your liking. Whisk the honey and orange zest and juice together and brush half of the mixture over the carrots. Return to the oven and roast for 10 minutes longer, or until the carrots are crisp-tender.

3   To serve, arrange the carrots on a platter, drizzle with the remaining orange mixture, and sprinkle with the mint.

Calories 55 • Total Fat 2g • Saturated Fat 0g • Carbohydrates 10g
Protein 0.5g • Dietary Fiber 2g • Sodium 28mg

When is the last time you enjoyed a musical?

On September 3, 2006, the American Film Institute revealed the top 25 movie musicals of all time. Here is the entire list for all you musical mavens.

	FILM	YEAR	STUDIO
1	*Singin' in the Rain*	1952	MGM
2	*West Side Story*	1961	United Artists
3	*The Wizard of Oz*	1939	MGM
4	*The Sound of Music*	1965	Twentieth Century-Fox
5	*Cabaret*	1972	Allied Artists
6	*Mary Poppins*	1964	Disney
7	*A Star Is Born*	1954	Warner Bros.
8	*My Fair Lady*	1964	Warner Bros.
9	*An American in Paris*	1951	MGM
10	*Meet Me in St. Louis*	1944	MGM
11	*The King and I*	1956	Twentieth Century-Fox
12	*Chicago*	2002	Miramax
13	*42nd Street*	1933	Warner Bros.
14	*All That Jazz*	1979	Twentieth Century-Fox
15	*Top Hat*	1935	RKO
16	*Funny Girl*	1968	Columbia

	FILM	YEAR	STUDIO
17	*The Band Wagon*	1953	MGM
18	*Yankee Doodle Dandy*	1942	Warner Bros.
19	*On the Town*	1949	MGM
20	*Grease*	1978	Paramount
21	*Seven Brides for Seven Brothers*	1954	MGM
22	*Beauty and the Beast*	1991	Disney
23	*Guys and Dolls*	1955	MGM
24	*Show Boat*	1936	Universal
25	*Moulin Rouge!*	2001	Twentieth Century Fox

WOULD SOMEONE JUST TELL ME . . .

Q: Can my lifestyle reduce my risk of breast cancer?

A: The medical community is taking action to address the finding that excess body weight is related to a diagnosis of cancer. It is now estimated that over 30 percent of all cancers could be prevented by lifestyle choices, according to the World Health Organization.

Researchers are not exactly sure *why* breast cancer survivors suffer weight gain as a side effect of treatment; but it may be due to treatment-related metabolic changes, sedentary lifestyles, menopause, long-term antihormone treatment, and any combination of these factors.

Increasing awareness of these issues will help postmenopausal women, in particular, avoid unhealthy weight gain that also increases the risk of primary breast cancer. In addition, physicians need to communicate the things that everyone can do to achieve and maintain a healthy lifestyle that minimizes the risk of recurrence.

An archeologist is the best husband a woman can have; the older she gets, the more interested he is in her.

~Agatha Christie

CHAPTER SIX

Soups, Stews, Risottos, and More

Optimistic

"Philosophy is perfectly right in saying that life must be understood backward. But then one forgets the other clause—it must be lived forward."

~Søren Kierkegaard

TGIF! Thank goodness it's Friday! These words have become embedded in our culture as we look forward to the end of the week.

But why think of one day as being better than another? Every day is essentially a neutral blank piece of paper. We impose on it any meaning we choose.

Just as everything else in our lives, each day revolves around how we feel, and our feelings determine our thoughts. So, if you are feeling in need of comfort, try to make changes to improve your mood or alter the situation, so you don't get stuck. Maybe seek out our resources of support (see pages 240–242), such as a licensed clinical psychologist, social worker, support group, spiritual adviser, or medical provider who may be helpful.

The soups, stews, and risottos in this chapter are all about sharing and support—each is designed to be "takeable" to a gathering of friends and family or to nourish someone you love when she needs something hearty for sustenance . . . including yourself.

Vegetable Chili

This satisfying recipe, from nutritionist Leigh Wagner, makes a large batch—excellent for serving to a group of your favorite friends or family, or even taking to a neighbor as a gift from your heart to hers. The chili also freezes well, so you can savor it again and again.

Makes 12 cups; serves 12 • Prep Time: 20 minutes • Cook Time: 30 minutes

1   tablespoon **olive oil**

2   large **onions**, chopped

1   medium green **bell pepper**, chopped

3   cloves **garlic**, minced

½   cup water

2   medium **carrots** or **sweet potatoes**, cut into chunks (¾ to 1 cup)

2   medium russet or **sweet potatoes**, cubed

2   cups **vegetable broth**

2   tablespoons **chili powder**

1   tablespoon **agave nectar**, **raw honey**, or **pure maple syrup**

1   teaspoon ground cumin

1   teaspoon dried **oregano**

1   teaspoon salt

½   teaspoon black pepper

¼   teaspoon cayenne pepper

1   small **zucchini**, sliced ¼ inch thick

1   small **yellow squash**, sliced ¼ inch thick

2   (28-ounce) cans diced **tomatoes**, with juice

⅓   cup **tomato sauce**

1   (15-ounce) can **kidney beans**, drained and rinsed

1   (15-ounce) can **garbanzo beans**, drained and rinsed

1   (15-ounce) can **black beans**, drained and rinsed

1   (15-ounce) can **black-eyed peas** or **other beans**, drained and rinsed

1   In a large soup pot, heat the oil over medium heat. Sauté the onions, bell pepper, and garlic for about 4 minutes, until tender. Add the water and carrots, cover, and cook over medium-low heat for 5 minutes. Add the potatoes, broth, chili powder, sweetener, cumin, oregano, salt, black pepper, and cayenne pepper, cover, and cook for 10 minutes.

2   Add the zucchini, squash, tomatoes, and tomato sauce and bring to a boil. Reduce the heat, cover, and simmer for 15 minutes. Add the kidney beans, garbanzo beans, black beans, and black-eyed peas and simmer for 30 minutes, or until the chili has thickened and the flavors have blended.

Calories 160 • Total Fat 2g • Saturated Fat 0g • Carbohydrates 29g
Protein 7g • Dietary Fiber 5g • Sodium 390mg

Orange-Tomato Gazpacho

When your garden or the farmer's market is in full swing, make this delicious cold soup for the flavor of summer. It revives, refreshes, and restores. Crèma (Mexican sour cream) is available in grocery stores that carry Hispanic food products; you can also use nonfat Greek yogurt.

Serves 4 • Prep Time: 20 minutes

1   pound ripe **tomatoes**, peeled and finely chopped

½   cup peeled and finely chopped seedless cucumber

1   red **bell pepper**, seeded and diced (see page 109)

1   small **red onion**, finely chopped

2   cups diced light wheat bread (from about 4 slices, crust removed)

2   tablespoons fresh lime juice

     Zest and juice of 1 **orange**

2   tablespoons extra-virgin **olive oil**

1   clove **garlic**, minced

¼   teaspoon ground cumin

     Salt and pepper

     Crèma or sour cream, for garnish

½   cup chopped fresh cilantro, for garnish

1. Place the tomatoes in a large glass bowl. Stir in the cucumber, bell pepper, onion, bread, lime juice, orange zest and juice, olive oil, garlic, and cumin. Season to taste with salt and pepper. Let stand at room temperature for 1 hour to release the vegetable juices.

2. To serve, spoon the gazpacho into bowls or cups. Dollop with crèma and sprinkle with cilantro.

Calories 168 • Total Fat 8g • Saturated Fat 1g • Carbohydrates 21g
Protein 4.5g • Dietary Fiber 3g • Sodium 139mg

Pet an animal to smooth out life's wrinkles.

Therapists have been known to prescribe a pet as a way of dealing with and recovering from depression. No one loves you more unconditionally than your pet. And a pet will listen to you talk all day long!

Zen Bowl

Sometimes being transported can be more a state of mind than a sense of place. Many Japanese start their day with a miso soup like this one. Miso is a living food, like an artisanal cheese. So buy it in the refrigerated section of a good grocery or health food store, then use it quickly or store in the refrigerator. This recipe is adapted from one by Susan Spungen.

Serves 4 • Prep Time: 20 minutes • Cook Time: 5 minutes

2 teaspoons **grapeseed oil** or canola oil

½ cup finely chopped **onion**

1 medium **carrot**, shredded

1 rib celery, finely chopped

4 cups low-sodium vegetable broth, such as Pacific

1 medium **carrot**, cut into thin coins

6 **shiitake mushrooms**, stems discarded, caps thinly sliced

3 tablespoons **red miso**

8 ounces finely diced cooked **chicken breast** or small peeled and deveined **shrimp**

2 sheets toasted **nori** (dried packaged **seaweed**), cut with scissors into ½-inch strips

Snipped fresh **chives**

1 Heat the oil in a large saucepan over medium-high heat. Sauté the onion, shredded carrot, and celery for 8 to 10 minutes, until softened. Stir in the broth, carrot coins, and mushrooms and cook for 10 minutes longer.

2 Reduce the heat to a simmer. Place the miso in a small bowl and ladle some of the hot broth over it. Using a spoon, break up the miso and blend with the broth. Return the miso broth to the saucepan and add the chicken or shrimp. Simmer for 1 minute (or until the shrimp turn pink), but do not boil.

3 To serve, ladle the soup into bowls and garnish with nori strips and fresh chives. You can cover and refrigerate any leftovers. To reheat, gently bring the soup just to a simmer, to keep the quality of the miso.

Calories 50 • Total Fat 1g • Saturated Fat 0g • Carbohydrates 5g • Protein 4g
Dietary Fiber 0.5g • Sodium 400mg

WHO KNEW?

Q: What is miso?

A: Miso is a fermented soy paste that the Japanese have used as a flavoring base since medieval times. It can be sweet, salty, earthy, fruity, and savory:

White miso: A sweet-tasting, lighter miso made from rice, barley, and soybeans. Use it in salad dressings and Asian sauces for vegetables and fish.

Yellow miso: An earthy-tasting miso made from soybeans, barley, and rice. Use it in dipping sauces, soups, and marinades.

Red miso: An aged miso, tasting savory and salty, made from soybeans. This has a deep umami flavor similar to soy sauce and is good in savory soups.

Where you exercise matters.

In September 2011, researchers at the University of Kansas Sport & Exercise Psychology Lab presented the results of a study demonstrating that the environment in fitness centers where people exercise has an important impact on their motivational responses.

For example, a recent survey with Jazzercise® participants revealed that they find the environment at Jazzercise centers to be very positive, supportive, and focused on each member's personal effort and improvement. Perceiving the environment in this way was linked with having more fun, trying harder, feeling more confident, and being more committed to engage in regular exercise.

Be kind to yourself . . . be as gentle and patient with yourself as you would be with your best friend.

~Cindy Himmelberg, art director

Mushroom and Broccoli Risotto

Reinvent the broccoli rice casserole with an easy, stir together risotto to which you can also add cooked chicken or firm tofu to make a one-dish meal. For the best flavor, use vegetable broth in a box, such as the Pacific brand. You can use any type of fresh mushrooms, but why not try a new variety? Maiitake mushrooms look like cream and brown peonies (see photo page 215). They should be somewhat moist yet firm to the touch, but not dry and brittle. Although they can be pricey, you need only 6 to 8 ounces for this dish. To prepare mushrooms, wipe them off with a moistened paper towel, then chop. Arborio, or other short grain Italian rice, is the classic risotto rice. Note: Add 2 cups chopped cooked chicken or vegetable protein for the last 5 minutes of cooking, if you wish.

Serves 4, 1-cup servings • Prep Time: 15 minutes • Cook Time: 20 minutes

2 tablespoons **olive oil**

1 clove **garlic**, minced

½ cup finely chopped yellow **onion**

3 cups chopped **maiitake mushrooms**, or a mix of maiitake, shiitake, button, or other fresh **mushrooms**

1 cup chopped **broccoli** florets

1 teaspoon fresh **thyme** leaves (optional)

5 cups **vegetable broth**

2 cups Arborio **rice**

¼ cup finely grated **Parmesan cheese**

Fresh thyme sprigs, for garnish

1 Heat 1 tablespoon of the oil in a large skillet over medium-high heat. Sauté the garlic, onion, mushrooms, broccoli, and thyme, if using, stirring often, for about 5 minutes, until the mushrooms and broccoli have softened and started to brown. Set aside.

continued on next page

DID YOU HEAR THE NEWS?

An Honest-to-Goodness Day's Work!

Have you ever felt exhilarated after a good day's work? Research suggests that working under pressure can actually give us a natural high. When we find ourselves in stressful circumstances, our brain releases certain chemicals that prepare our body to cope with that situation.

First, the hormones adrenaline and noradrenaline are released into our body, increasing our heart rate, bringing more oxygen to our lungs, and releasing a surge of energy. This process temporarily boosts our energy, gives us temporary muscle power, forces us to breathe in a short and shallow way, and allows our body to move quickly and our minds to reach an instant decision. Adrenaline and other feel-good chemicals called serotonin and endorphins flood our body, giving us a sense of achievement and high spirits.

2 In a medium saucepan, heat the broth until it begins to bubble; maintain at a simmer. In a large saucepan, heat the remaining 1 tablespoon oil over medium-high heat. Stir in the rice, and cook, stirring, for 1 to 2 minutes, until the rice begins to turn opaque white.

3 Ladle in 2 cups of the hot broth and continue to stir until the rice absorbs the broth. Add 1 more cup broth and continue to stir until the rice absorbs the broth. Transfer the mushroom mixture to the rice and add the remaining 2 cups broth. Continue to stir for 10 to 12 minutes, until the risotto thickens and the rice is soft, yet a little firm when you bite a rice kernel. Stir in the cheese. Serve right away or cover and chill, then warm in the oven until heated through. To serve, spoon onto plates and top each with a fresh thyme sprig.

Calories 112 • Total Fat 7g • Saturated Fat 1.5g
Carbohydrates 9g • Protein 4g • Dietary Fiber 1g
Sodium 400mg

Have-It-All Chili

What could be better than chocolate in chili? What a fantastic way to get a depth of flavor and color. For a weekend get-together, tailgating, or a cozy fireside supper, this vegetarian treat will make meat lovers happy, too. You don't expect fruit in chili, but somehow it all works, while keeping that deep, spicy chili flavor we all love.

Serves 4 • Prep Time: 10 minutes • Cook Time: 40 minutes

½ cup chopped **onion**

1 clove **garlic**, crushed

1 (14.5-ounce) can diced **tomatoes**, with juice

1 (14-ounce) can **vegetable broth** or chicken broth

1 (8-ounce) can **tomato sauce**

1 green or red **bell pepper**, seeded and chopped (see page 109)

1 tart **apple**, peeled, cored, and chopped

1 tablespoon **chili powder**

1½ teaspoons unsweetened **cocoa powder**

½ teaspoon ground **cinnamon**

1 (15-ounce) can **kidney beans**, drained and rinsed

¼ cup almonds, whole, chopped, or slivered

¼ cup dried apricots, chopped

Salt and pepper

1 cup shredded Cheddar cheese, for garnish

1 In a large saucepan, combine the onion, garlic, tomatoes, broth, tomato sauce, bell pepper, apple, chili powder, cocoa powder, and cinnamon. Over medium-high heat, bring to a boil, reduce the heat, and simmer for 30 minutes.

2 Stir in the beans, almonds, and apricots and simmer for 10 minutes. Taste for seasoning, then serve in bowls. Garnish each bowl with cheese and serve.

Calories 200 • Total Fat 2g • Saturated Fat 1g • Carbohydrates 20g
Protein 7g • Dietary Fiber 4g • Sodium 400mg

Be prepared to take life minute by minute in the beginning of a crisis. It will gradually spread to hour by hour, day by day, week to week.

~Anonymous

DID YOU HEAR THE NEWS?

The Power of Your Smile

New research is suggesting that we can affect enormous positive changes in our lives and in the lives of others by using a tool that we always have with us: our smiles.

This process is called *emotional contagion*. Feeling good is contagious, and so is feeling bad.

According to a report in the January 2000 issue of *Psychological Science*, research from Lund University in Sweden revealed that mimicking a person's bodily state or facial expression causes physical responses in the receiver's body that are identical to those in the sender's. Therefore, when you smile at someone else, they smile and you are causing physiological changes within their bodies. Frequent smiling has many therapeutic and health benefits, particularly when the smile is a Duchenne smile. According to Mark Stibich, PhD, a health behavior specialist, smiling:

- Boosts the immune system

- Increases positive affect

- Reduces stress

- Lowers blood pressure

- Enhances other people's perception of you

Is your smile real?

Duchenne smiles are marked by wrinkles in the eyes that resemble crow's feet and are associated with feelings of excitement, amusement, interest, happiness, and joy.

A well-known study of Duchenne smiles, conducted at the University of California, Berkeley, and published in a 2001 issue of the *Journal of Personality and Social Psychology*, demonstrated the impact of smiling on life satisfaction. Researchers analyzed the yearbook pictures of 111 smiling women at age twenty-one, fifty of whom displayed authentic Duchenne smiles. Participants expressing genuine positive emotions in their yearbook picture were more likely to be married and have higher well-being than their non–Duchenne smiling classmates. This study was replicated in Australia in 2006 and demonstrated similar results.

PROFESSOR POSITIVE

The Pursuit of Happiness

Sometimes it feels selfish to focus so much on trying to be joyful, but it's actually good for you. A review of dozens of research studies titled "Positive Affect and Health," by Sheldon Cohen and Sarah D. Pressman, was published in the 2006 issue of *Current Directions in Psychological Science*. The results showed that positive emotions or affect (defined here as "feelings that reflect a level of pleasurable engagement with the environment, such as happiness, joy, excitement, enthusiasm, and contentment") are associated with a range of better general health outcomes. These range from years of additional life to a decreased likelihood of catching the common cold. Treat the pursuit of happiness the way you treat exercising: It is a health-promoting behavior!

Tuscan Ribollita

If you've ever dreamed of—or actually been to—Cortona, the Tuscan town made famous by Frances Mayes's book *Under the Tuscan Sun*, then you know about this robust one-dish meal. Ribollita is a minestrone-like soup that includes hearty greens and toasted, cheese-topped bread for body and flavor.

Serves 8 • Prep Time: 15 minutes • Cook Time: 50 minutes

8 small slices Whole Wheat and **Flaxseed** Boule (page 120) or store-bought Italian bread

½ cup grated **Parmesan** or **Asiago cheese**

2 tablespoons **olive oil**

1 large yellow **onion**, chopped

3 cloves **garlic**, minced

2 **carrots**, chopped

2 ribs celery, chopped

2 teaspoons chopped fresh **rosemary**

2 cups fresh or thawed frozen cubed **butternut squash**

1 cup canned diced **tomatoes**

5 cups chicken broth or **vegetable broth**

3 cups chopped **kale** leaves, stems cut out

1 (15-ounce) can **cannellini beans**, drained and rinsed

Salt and freshly ground black pepper

1 For the toasted bread, preheat the oven to 350°F. Arrange the bread slices on a large baking sheet. Sprinkle the top of each slice with 1 tablespoon of the cheese. Bake for 20 minutes, or until the edges of the bread have browned and the cheese is browned and bubbling. Remove from the oven and let cool.

2 Meanwhile, for the soup, heat the oil in a large saucepan over medium-high heat. Sauté the onion, garlic, carrots, and celery for 8 to 10 minutes, until softened. Stir in the rosemary, squash, tomatoes, broth, and kale and bring to a boil. Cook, covered, for 30 minutes, or until the squash is tender. Add the beans and simmer for 10 minutes, until the flavors have blended. Season to taste with salt and pepper.

3 To serve, place 1 toast in the bottom of each bowl and ladle with soup. Serve hot.

Calories 70 • Total Fat 3g • Saturated Fat 0.5g • Carbohydrates 20g
Protein 5g • Dietary Fiber 1.5g • Sodium 400mg

When a person is diagnosed with cancer, I believe that it is important for her to remember that cancer is a part of life . . . and not life itself.

~Catie Knight, MPH, Survivorship Health Coordinator

Everyone's Velvet Cream of Potato Soup

You'll adore this creative way to use cauliflower; it's perfect for those who love creamy soups, but not the fat. Leeks, green onions, and shallots are different members of the onion family, but tender green onions have a much stronger onion flavor than the tougher leek, which is somewhat sweet. The leeks, garlic, and bay leaf help build flavor in a gentle way.

Serves 4 • Prep Time: 15 minutes • Cook Time: 30 minutes

1 tablespoon **olive oil** or **grapeseed oil**

2 **leeks**, white only, chopped

1 clove **garlic**, minced

1 bay leaf

2 large russet potatoes, peeled and cubed

1 small head **cauliflower**, core removed, florets cut into small pieces

6 cups **vegetable broth** or chicken broth

Salt and pepper

½ cup low fat **Greek yogurt**

2 tablespoons chopped fresh Italian **parsley** or snipped **chives**

1 Heat the oil in a large saucepan over medium-high heat. Sauté the leeks for about 8 minutes, until tender. Add the garlic and sauté for 1 minute. Add the bay leaf, potatoes, cauliflower, and broth. Bring to a boil, cover, then simmer for 20 minutes, or until the potatoes and cauliflower are tender.

2 To serve, remove the bay leaf and season to taste. Ladle into bowls and top with a dollop of yogurt and a sprinkle of parsley.

Calories 70 • Total Fat 3g • Saturated Fat 0.5g • Carbohydrates 20g
Protein 5g • Dietary Fiber 1.5g • Sodium 400mg

Roasted Tomato Basil Soup

Since tomatoes are so good for us, why not make the best-ever "cream" of tomato soup? This one has a depth of umami flavor from the anchovies, which just melt into the soup. Or, if you like, use anchovy paste from a tube. If you prefer a vegetarian or vegan version, use 2 teaspoons soy sauce in place of the anchovies. The touch of sweetness is a medium-flavored honey made in summer when bees visit all the wildflowers. Adapted from a recipe by Chef Charles d'Ablaing.

Serves 6 • Prep Time: 15 minutes • Cook Time: 45 minutes

6 cups Roma **tomatoes**, cut in half lengthwise (about 4 pounds)

2 tablespoons **olive oil**

½ cup diced **red onion**

2 cloves **garlic**, minced

3 canned **anchovy fillets**, or 2 teaspoons **anchovy paste** or **soy sauce**

¼ cup wildflower or clover **honey**

½ cup **red wine** or vegetable broth

¼ cup fresh **basil** leaves, chopped

Salt and pepper

1 Preheat the oven to 375°F. Line 2 rimmed baking sheets with parchment paper or aluminum foil and coat with a small amount of oil or butter. Place the tomatoes on the prepared pans, cut side down, and roast for 10 to 15 minutes, until the skins begin to wrinkle and are easily pulled off.

2 Meanwhile, heat the olive oil in a large saucepan over medium heat. Cook the onion, garlic, and anchovy fillets, stirring, for about 7 minutes, until the onion is tender. Stir in the honey and wine and cook for 10 minutes.

3 Add the roasted tomatoes and basil and simmer for 15 minutes, or until the flavors have blended . Remove from the heat and puree, in batches, in a food processor or with an immersion blender. Season to taste.

Calories 181 • Total Fat 5g • Saturated Fat 0.5g • Carbohydrates 30g
Protein 1g • Dietary Fiber 1g • Sodium 137mg

Oaxacan Chicken in Mole

Conquered by the Aztecs in 1482 and by the Spanish in 1522, Oaxaca is a province known for the variety of its moles (pronounced mole-ay), sauces made by grinding many ingredients together. Chicken slowly simmered in a spicy mole becomes fall-apart tender as well as uniquely flavored. Serve this dish over cooked rice. Many grocery and big box stores now stock Mexican ingredients. You can find ground dried chiles in the spice section or Hispanic section of your grocery store. Note: Cooking about 1⅓ cups rice will give you the 4 cups cooked rice you'll need for serving the mole.

Serves 4 • Prep Time: 25 minutes • Cook Time: 1 hour

2 tablespoons ground dried ancho **chile**

½ cup whole blanched almonds

¼ cup diced green plantain or **bananas**

1 teaspoon ground **cinnamon**

1 clove **garlic**

4 soft (6-inch) corn tortillas, torn into pieces

2 tablespoons roasted pumpkin seeds

1 to 1½ ounces Mexican **chocolate** or semisweet chocolate

3½ cups chicken broth or vegetable broth

1 cup canned diced **tomatoes**, with juice

Salt

1 pound boneless, skinless **chicken thighs**, or 12 ounces firm **tofu**

1 large **onion**, sliced

2 cloves **garlic**, chopped

4 cups hot cooked **rice**

Chopped fresh cilantro, for garnish

1 For the mole, puree the ground chile, almonds, plantain, cinnamon, garlic, tortilla pieces, pumpkin seeds, and chocolate with 1 cup of the broth in a food processor until blended but still grainy. Pour the mixture into a saucepan, add 1 cup more of the broth and the tomatoes, and bring to a simmer, stirring, over medium heat. Cook, stirring, for about 5 minutes, until the chocolate melts and the flavors have blended. Season to taste with salt. The mole will keep, covered, in the refrigerator for up to 3 days.

2 Place the chicken pieces in a large saucepan. Add the onion, garlic, and the remaining 1½ cups broth, and bring to a boil. Reduce the heat to a simmer. Cook, covered, for 45 minutes, or until the chicken is tender and cooked through. (For tofu, simply combine the cubed tofu with the mole mixture.) Stir in the mole and bring to a boil over medium-high heat. To serve, ladle the chicken in mole over hot rice and sprinkle with cilantro.

Calories 250 • Total Fat 5g • Saturated Fat 1g
Carbohydrates 50g • Protein 20g • Dietary Fiber 2g
Sodium 250mg

What Peter Pumpkin Knew about Pumpkin Seeds

Phytosterols are compounds found in plants that have a chemical structure very similar to cholesterol. Laboratory studies suggest that phytosterols reduce blood levels of cholesterol and enhance our immune systems when they are present in our diet in sufficient amounts. Phytosterols are currently being studied to determine their ability to decrease the risk of certain cancers.

In a study in the November 2005 *Journal of Agricultural and Food Chemistry*, researchers published the amounts of phytosterols present in nuts and seeds commonly eaten in the United States. Of the nuts and seeds typically consumed as snack foods, pistachios and sunflower seeds were richest in phytosterols, closely followed by pumpkin seeds.

The beneficial effects of phytosterols are so dramatic they have been extracted from soybean, corn, and pine tree oil and added to processed foods, such as butter-replacement spreads, which are then touted as cholesterol-lowering "foods."

Cauliflower and Saffron Risotto

Adapted from a recipe by David Rosengarten, this stirring risotto (pun intended) features powerhouse cauliflower as well as saffron and turmeric, which help create the golden broth. Sometimes just stirring the pot, focusing on that moment and inhaling the savory aroma, is invigorating. Arborio is a short grain Italian rice available at most grocery stores; if you can't find it, no problem . . . just use any short grain rice. You can find saffron threads in the spice aisle of better grocery stores.

Serves 4 • Prep Time: 15 minutes • Cook Time: 15 minutes

6	cups low-sodium chicken broth or vegetable broth
1	tablespoon **olive oil**
1	medium **onion**, chopped
1	cup Arborio or other short grain **rice**
¼	teaspoon **saffron threads**
¼	teaspoon ground **turmeric**
2	cups small (1-inch) **cauliflower** florets
	Salt and freshly ground black pepper
½	cup freshly grated **Parmesan cheese**

1 In a medium saucepan, bring the broth to a gentle simmer. In a large saucepan, heat the oil over medium-high heat. Sauté the onion for about 4 minutes, until transparent. Stir in the rice, saffron, and turmeric and stir for 1 minute to coat the rice. Stir in the cauliflower.

2 Ladle in 1 cup of the broth and cook, stirring, until the desired degree of absorption is reached. Keep adding the broth, 1 cup at a time, stirring until absorbed, for about 10 minutes, until all the broth has been used and the rice is tender. Season to taste. To serve, ladle the risotto into bowls and top with grated Parmesan.

Calories 200 • Total Fat 2g • Saturated Fat 1g • Carbohydrates 20g
Protein 7g • Dietary Fiber 4g • Sodium 400mg

DID YOU HEAR THE NEWS?

Wild about saffron!

Saffron is the little thread at the center of a small purple crocus flower, where pollen catches and develops. Rare and hard to cultivate because there are only three per flower, these threads are handpicked and dried before they are sold. Saffron is the world's most expensive spice because it takes a lot of effort to harvest, and more than thirteen thousand threads are required to make just a single ounce of saffron.

Saffron can be purchased in powder form or in thread form. Buyer beware: Buying saffron threads may be the best option because ground saffron is often mixed with other spices, meaning that you could buy diluted saffron but pay for the real deal!

ON THE UPSWING

Life is a balancing act.

Food is meant to sustain our bodies but also can provide pleasure and, at times, may also be used as a coping mechanism. "We learned our eating behaviors long ago. Changing these behaviors requires planning, paying attention to our emotions around food, and making mindful choices. We are best served by balancing our choices and getting rid of "all or nothing" thinking.

Every day, I am told by patients, "Well, I messed up in the morning. So the whole day was blown, and I just went with it." The problem with this statement is "all or nothing" thinking. The choices we make are moment to moment; getting in the habit of thinking with purpose and being mindful of our environment and ourselves will become easier, as we practice these behaviors each day.

~Jennifer Klemp, PhD, MPH, The Breast Cancer Survivorship Center, University of Kansas Cancer Center

Roasted Spaghetti Squash with Tomatoes, Kale, and Herbs

Growing ever more popular, spaghetti squash has a sweet flavor and a tender interior that, once cooked until tender, you can remove with a fork and toss like spaghetti. If you prefer, you can roast the squash and tomatoes up to a day ahead of time, then heat them with the sautéed kale. Sprinkle with Pecorino or other hard grating cheese, such as Parmesan or Romano, then serve as a main course, toss with cooked pasta, or enjoy as a side dish.

Serves 4 • Prep Time: 15 minutes • Cook Time: 1 hour

2 tablespoons **olive oil**

2 spaghetti **squash**

8 Roma **tomatoes**

3 large cloves **garlic**, minced

¼ teaspoon dried **red pepper flakes**

1 head **kale**, stems removed and leaves chopped

1 teaspoon dried **oregano**

2 tablespoons dry white wine or **vegetable broth**

Salt and pepper

2 tablespoons grated **Pecorino**, **Romano**, or **Parmesan cheese**

1 Preheat the oven to 400°F and line two large rimmed baking sheets with aluminum foil. Place 1 tablespoon of oil in a large nonstick skillet. Using a pastry brush, lightly brush the foil with a little of the oil. Cut the squash in half lengthwise and scoop out the seeds. Place the squash, flesh side down, on the prepared pans. Roast for 30 minutes.

2 Cut the Roma tomatoes in half lengthwise. Remove the pans from the oven and place the tomatoes, cut side down, around the squash. Return to the oven and roast for 20 minutes longer, or until the squash is tender when pierced with a fork and the tomato skins have shriveled. When cool enough to handle, use a fork to scoop out the strands of squash. Peel off the tomato skins. Use the squash and tomatoes right away, or cover and refrigerate until ready to finish the dish.

continued on next page

The Surprising Impact of Kale

Researchers have found that the cruciferous family of vegetables (also known as "brassica"), including kale, cabbage, broccoli, turnips, and Brussels sprouts, may help protect against cancer due to naturally occurring chemicals that disrupt the cancer-forming process. (See the Beller Nutritional Institute report, page 149.)

Kale is also good for your bones because it is a great source of calcium and high in vitamin K. The calcium in kale is more absorbable than the calcium in milk, which makes it an even more powerful protector against osteoporosis (a common side effect of some kinds of breast cancer treatments). Vitamin K has been demonstrated to reduce the rate of bone loss in postmenopausal women.

3 To finish the dish, heat the remaining olive oil in the skillet over medium-high heat. Add the garlic and red pepper flakes, then the kale. Sauté for about 8 minutes, until the kale is emerald green and crisp-tender. Stir in the oregano and wine until well combined. Then stir in the squash and tomatoes. Toss the squash, tomatoes, and kale mixture together like pasta. Season to taste.

4 Serve in shallow bowls and top each with ½ tablespoon cheese.

Calories 164 • Total Fat 9g • Saturated Fat 1.5g
Carbohydrates 19g • Protein 6g • Dietary Fiber 4g
Sodium 110mg

WHO KNEW?

Q: How do I buy a spaghetti squash?

A: Averaging 4 to 8 pounds, the cylinder-shaped spaghetti squash is generally available year-round with a peak season from early fall through winter. While a true spaghetti squash is pale ivory to pale yellow in color, an orange spaghetti squash, known as Orangetti, is higher in beta carotene and a little sweeter than the paler variety. A low-calorie vegetable, spaghetti squash has just 37 calories in a four-ounce serving loaded with nutrition.

Cheese Tortellini with Artichoke-Roasted Red Pepper Sauce

With pasta ingredients on hand in your freezer, refrigerator, and kitchen cupboards, you can have this big flavor meal ready in under 30 minutes. The sauce is also good over fish or chicken.

Serves 4 • Prep Time: 15 minutes • Cook Time: 15 minutes

16 ounces frozen, or 8 to 9 ounces dried, cheese tortellini

2 tablespoons **olive oil**

2 cloves **garlic**, minced

1 (12-ounce) jar roasted **red peppers**, drained and rinsed, finely chopped

1 (12-ounce) jar marinated **artichoke** hearts, drained and rinsed, finely chopped

½ cup chopped fresh **basil**

1. Bring a large pot of salted water to a boil. Add the tortellini and cook according to the package directions.

2. Meanwhile, heat the oil over medium-high heat in a large skillet and sauté the garlic, red peppers, and artichoke hearts, stirring occasionally, for 4 to 5 minutes, until the mixture forms a chunky sauce.

3. Remove the tortellini with a slotted spoon and add to the sauce. Gently toss, adding some of the pasta cooking water, if necessary. Serve topped with basil.

Calories 299 • Total Fat 14g • Saturated Fat 4.5g • Carbohydrates 33g
Protein 11g • Dietary Fiber 6g • Sodium 166mg

I started living rather than worrying about what lies ahead.

~Donna Pelletier, cancer survivorship advocate

Orzo with Spinach, Garbanzo Beans, and Feta

When you get home and are hungry for something comforting and quick, orzo pasta is your friend. The small, tear-shaped pasta cooks in about 8 minutes. Then, it's ready to toss with the other ready-to-go ingredients for a colorful, savory, filling, good-for-you meal. Any leftovers make a great cold pasta salad the next day.

Serves 4 • Prep Time: 10 minutes • Cook Time: 15 minutes

1½ ounces orzo pasta, cooked according to package directions (about 2 cups cooked)

1 (15-ounce) can **garbanzo beans**, drained and rinsed

2 cups baby **spinach**

¼ cup crumbled feta cheese (about 1 ounce)

1 tablespoon **olive oil**

2 teaspoons fresh **lemon juice**

1 clove **garlic**, minced

Salt and pepper

1 Stir the pasta, garbanzo beans, spinach, and cheese together in a large bowl. In a small bowl, whisk the olive oil, lemon juice, and garlic together, pour over the pasta, and toss to blend. Season to taste. Serve warm, at room temperature, or chilled.

Calories 280 • Total Fat 8.5g • Saturated Fat 2g • Carbohydrates 39g
Protein 13g • Dietary Fiber 7.5g • Sodium 267mg

Revved Up Mac and Cheese

With whole grain macaroni, cauliflower, and butternut squash, this home-cooking classic gets the update it needs to truly comfort us, while keeping the flavor of traditional mac 'n' cheese. To save time, simply mash canned butternut squash or sweet potatoes.

Serves 8 • Prep Time: 15 minutes • Cook Time: 35 minutes

1   cup whole grain elbow macaroni

1   tablespoon **grapeseed oil** or **canola oil**

1   clove **garlic**, minced

¼   cup diced **onion**

1   cup finely chopped fresh or thawed frozen **cauliflower**

1   bay leaf

½   teaspoon freshly ground black pepper

2   tablespoons cornstarch

2   cups 2% **milk**

½   cup mashed **butternut squash** or sweet potatoes

1   teaspoon Worcestershire sauce or **soy sauce**

½   teaspoon dried mustard

1   teaspoon garlic powder

¾   teaspoon salt

¼   teaspoon **apple cider vinegar**

1   cup shredded Cheddar cheese (about 4 ounces)

2   tablespoons grated **Parmesan cheese**

¼   cup whole wheat bread crumbs

1   Preheat the oven to 425°F. Coat a 9-inch round baking dish with a small amount of butter or oil.

2   Cook the macaroni according to the package directions. Drain and toss with a little oil to prevent sticking. Set aside. In a medium saucepan, heat the oil over medium-high heat. Sauté the garlic and onion for about 7 minutes, until golden. Stir in the cauliflower and cook, stirring, for about 4 minutes, until the cauliflower begins to brown. Stir in the bay leaf and pepper.

3   In a medium bowl, whisk the cornstarch and milk together. Pour into the onion mixture and cook, stirring, for 2 to 3 minutes, until thickened. Stir in the squash, Worcestershire sauce, mustard, garlic powder, salt, and vinegar. Add the cheeses and stir until melted. Remove the bay leaf and stir in the cooked macaroni until well blended. Spoon the macaroni mixture into the prepared pan and top with the bread crumbs.

4   Bake for 20 to 25 minutes, until the bread crumbs are golden brown and the edges of the macaroni are bubbling.

Calories 198 • Total Fat 8.5g • Saturated Fat 4g • Carbohydrates 22g
Protein 9g • Dietary Fiber 2g • Sodium 430 mg

Meditation goes mainstream.

It is important to fill yourself up . . . I learned to receive the love and support of others and give time and attention to my "self."

~Carol LaRue, author and occupational therapist

Meditation and relaxation . . . even the words themselves sound good. Although controlled research on meditation/relaxation is relatively recent, there is considerable evidence documenting its stress reduction benefits.

According to an article in *Brain Behavior and Immunity* in August 2008, preliminary research has shown that practicing mindfulness can lead to improved immune function, a higher quality of life, and better coping with stress in women newly diagnosed with early stage breast cancer.

The positive effects of mindfulness meditation on pain and memory may result from an "improved ability to regulate a crucial brain wave called the alpha rhythm," according to an April 21, 2011, news release from Massachusetts General Hospital, citing research reports from Massachusetts General Hospital, Harvard Medical School, and the Massachusetts Institute of Technology. A benefit of meditation may be this "turning down the volume" on distracting information, which helps the brain deal with overstimulation.

"Modulation of the alpha rhythm in response to attention-directing cues was faster and significantly more enhanced among study participants who completed an eight-week mindfulness meditation program than in a control group," according to the researchers.

The concept that the mind is important in the treatment of illness is integral to the healing approaches of traditional Chinese medicine and *ayurvedic medicine* as well, dating back more than two thousand years. Hippocrates also noted the moral and spiritual aspects of healing and thought that treatment could occur only with consideration of attitude, environmental influences, and natural remedies.

Meditation and relaxation have also been shown to be beneficial in the treatment of: postoperative, cancer-related, and chronic pain, and chronic insomnia. People use meditation to increase calmness, improve psychological balance, cope with illness, and enhance overall health and well-being.

Try this simple introduction to meditation from *YogaJournal.com*.

Sit comfortably in an upright but relaxed position. Close your eyes and bring your attention to your nostrils. As you breathe notice the subtle sensation of cool air passing into, and warm air passing out of, your nose. Without manipulating the breath, simply notice the sensation. Maintain your attention to every breath. Staying relaxed and mentally alert, become curious about each passing breath as if it were your first.

If your attention wanders, simply notice the distraction and patiently return to the sensation of the breath. Your ability to stay present deepens by consistently returning to the current moment.

Do this exercise for 10 minutes once or twice a day, gradually extending your sessions to 20 or 30 minutes each.

PROFESSOR POSITIVE

Take a deep breath!

You may not realize it, but many people breathe incorrectly, especially during times of stress. Breathing incorrectly is not only a problem for your athletic activity, it can also lead to health problems, aches and pains, and fatigue. Believe it or not, six breaths per minute is considered optimal, according to a study published in *The Lancet* in May 1998.

Try counting your breaths on your own and you might be surprised to find out that you may be more than doubling this rate. Try closing your eyes and breathing more slowly and deeply with your belly for a few minutes. You will likely notice that you are in a more relaxed state. Slowing down your breathing not only reduces your heart rate but it also improves your heart rate variability. Both of these measures are tied to better health and relaxation, so take a deep breath!

Imagination is the highest
kite one can fly.

~Lauren Bacall

Adventurous

*"Don't refuse to go on an occasional wild goose chase.
That's what wild geese are for."*

~*Author unknown*

"The world is divided into two kinds of people: those who wake up thinking about what they are going to eat for supper and those who don't," according to *The Splendid Table's How to Eat Supper*, by Lynne Rosetto Kasper and Sally Swift.

Well, we make up a third kind. We think about what to make for dinner both early in the morning and late in the afternoon, depending on the day of the week or the mood we're in . . . as we plan our days around work, family, and "to do" list entries.

So whatever time "make dinner" pops up on your mental list of "do's," we've got you covered. Knowing that you may choose from the breakfast, appetizers and snacks, or even the dessert chapter for inspiration, we share these more traditionally known dinner recipes when time in the kitchen is on your "to do" list, too. Many are a bit more complex than those in the other chapters, but, hey, we are all about mixing it up. One thing is certain: These protein-packed picks will keep your hunger in check all through the night.

Island Fish Tacos
with Fresh Pineapple Salsa

People who love fish tacos will make this amazing recipe a special part of the week. These fresh-tasting tacos are deliciously simple to make. Bringing the islands together with south of the border flavors creates a lovefest for your taste buds. The pineapple salsa is also good, on its own, with Baked Tortilla Chips (page 102).

Serves 6 • Prep Time: 30 minutes • Cook Time: 10 minutes

FRESH PINEAPPLE SALSA

2   cups chopped fresh **pineapple**

2   tablespoons fresh lime juice

½   cup chopped cilantro

1   jalapeño **chile**, seeded

½   teaspoon crushed **red pepper flakes**

    Salt

ISLAND FISH TACOS

½   head **red cabbage**, cored and thinly sliced

2   tablespoons **apple cider vinegar**

1   tablespoon **grapeseed oil**, **canola oil**, or **olive oil**, for brushing

    Salt and pepper

6   (6-ounce) skinless **halibut**, **yellow snapper**, or **cod** fillets

6   (10-inch) flour tortillas, warmed, for serving

1   medium ripe avocado, halved, pitted, peeled, and chopped

1 For the pineapple salsa, place the pineapple, lime juice, cilantro, chile, and red pepper flakes in a blender or food processor and pulse until somewhat smooth yet a little chunky. Season to taste with salt.

2 For the slaw, combine the red cabbage and vinegar in a medium bowl and season with salt.

3 Heat a nonstick skillet over medium-high heat. Brush the fish with oil, then season with salt and pepper. Measure the thickness of the fish (it's usually about ¾ inch). Cook the fish, turning once, for 10 minutes per 1 inch of thickness (about 7½ minutes for a ¾-inch-thick fillet), or until the fish begins to flake when tested with a fork in the thickest part.

4 To serve, cut the fish into strips and place in the tortillas. Garnish with the slaw, avocado, and pineapple salsa.

Calories 277 • Total Fat 10g • Saturated Fat 1.5g • Carbohydrates 38g Protein 11g • Dietary Fiber 5g • Sodium 322mg

Keeping Fatigue from Robbing You of Your Energy

A 2006 review of studies in the *European Journal of Cancer* found that as many as 19 to 38 percent of cancer patients experience "disabling fatigue." Mary Calys, PT, DPT, director of cancer rehabilitation and fatigue management at North Kansas City Hospital, notes that getting help for fatigue encourages cancer survivors to regain their strength and become functional once again.

Women receiving chemotherapy, or chemotherapy plus radiation, are more likely to experience fatigue than those who undergo radiation only. Fatigue can last long after treatment has been completed; up to 40 percent of patients report that fatigue still interferes with their lives three years or more after treatment. Share your symptoms of fatigue with your physician in order to rule out treatable causes, such as anemia, low oxygen in your blood, sleep apnea, or medications that need changes.

How do you recognize the symptoms of fatigue? What does it look like? Dr. Calys says that changes in sleep quality, cognition, stamina, emotional reactivity, control over body process (i.e, keeping the mind/body in sync), and social interaction may be the first signs that tiredness has progressed to fatigue or even exhaustion. When fatigue interferes with quality of life, impacts your health, or impedes your response to treatment—then it should be discussed with your physician or a clinician who has expertise in fatigue management strategies.

Here are some lifestyle tools to help fatigue fade away:

• EXERCISE MODERATELY. Ask your doctor how much exercise is safe for you. Getting rest is important, but physical activity has proven benefits—improving mood, conferring a general sense of well-being, and countering fatigue, as well as impacting cancer recurrence. Women who exercised regularly prior to their diagnosis will find it easier to return to working out; newcomers may need to focus on setting smaller goals, such as walking for fifteen minutes three days a week.

- GET ENOUGH SLEEP. Keep a journal noting how much you sleep and how you feel the next day, so you can know what amount of rest works for you. If you are having trouble sleeping, talk with your health care provider about your situation.

- KNOW YOUR EATING HABITS. Eating regular meals is very helpful when it comes to maintaining your baseline energy level. Avoid becoming too hungry or eating in excess. In addition, emphasizing whole-grain, low-fat, and lean protein-rich foods can prevent some of the highs and lows in your energy level.

- KEEP YOUR ENVIRONMENT COMFORTABLE. Setting the thermostat at a comfortable temperature—not too hot, not too cold—can help your energy level as well.

- KEEP A JOURNAL. Keeping a journal can help you identify times of the day when you have the most energy, so you can plan accordingly. It can also help identify those things that seem to drain your energy level, and activities that improve it.

- ASK YOUR HEALTH CARE PROVIDER ABOUT ACUPUNCTURE. In one very preliminary study at Memorial Sloan-Kettering Cancer Center, published in the May 2004 *Journal of Clinical Oncology*, acupuncture was shown to reduce postchemotherapy fatigue by 31 percent in people with various types of cancer. In 2005, early research demonstrated potential reductions in fatigue and hot flashes, but further research is needed. Another preliminary study of breast cancer patients in Sweden showed that acupuncture reduced hot flashes by half. While doctors find these results encouraging, they are still very early results and require further study. For more information, see page 229.

Note: Anyone who has had lymph nodes removed from under an arm should not have needles inserted into that arm. If acupuncture is used on the arm, there is a risk of lymphedema, swelling caused by an excess of fluid in the arm. Talk to the acupuncturist about other treatments that could be used on that arm, such as aromatherapy.

Ricotta and Parsley Gnocchi with Slow-Simmered Tomato Sauce with Red Wine

Gnocchi (NYOH-kee, NOH-kee), Italian for "dumplings," can be made from potatoes or flour. It's common for eggs or cheese to be added to the dough, plus finely chopped spinach is also popular. High-protein, low-carbohydrate, and all delicious, this pillowy pasta is stirred together in a bowl. You can form it into ropes, then cut, or take the quick route and simply drop teaspoonfuls of the mixture into boiling water. Sometimes, it feels good to work with this soft dough; other times, you just want to eat—quickly! With garlic, olive oil, red wine, and tomatoes in the sauce, you've got a delicious pasta dish that's good for you, too. If you buy a jarred marinara sauce, be sure it's low in sugar and free of preservatives.

Serves 4 • Prep Time: 25 minutes • Cook Time: 20 minutes

15 ounces low-fat ricotta

¼ cup plus 1 tablespoon all-purpose flour, plus more for dusting

¼ cup very finely chopped fresh Italian **parsley**

4 cups Slow-Simmered **Tomato** Sauce with **Red Wine** (recipe follows) or other marinara-style sauce, heated

1 Bring a large pot of salted water to a boil.

2 In a medium bowl, blend the ricotta with the flour and parsley until you have a firm but not stiff dough. To work by hand, transfer the dough to a floured surface. Divide into fourths and roll each fourth into a 1-inch wide rope, dusting with flour as necessary. Cut the rope into 1-inch pieces. Or use a very small scoop or a tablespoon to scoop out portions of dough. Drop into the boiling water, in batches. When the gnocchi float to the top, remove them with a slotted spoon to a plate or bowl and keep warm.

3 To serve, place 1 cup sauce on each plate and top with the gnocchi.

Calories 184 • Total Fat 8.5g • Saturated Fat 5g • Carbohydrates 13g
Protein 13g • Dietary Fiber 0g • Sodium 135mg

Slow-Simmered Tomato Sauce with Red Wine

On a weekend, make a big pot of this sauce. Enjoy it over pasta one night, then freeze the leftovers for easy weeknight meals to come. The combination of tomatoes, olive oil, and red wine is especially potent as it maximizes the lycopene your body can absorb. And the flavor is fabulous, too! The easiest way to chop tomatoes in a can is to carefully plunge your kitchen shears into an open can and start snipping. If you like, add browned ground turkey or texturized vegetable protein meatballs to the sauce after it is cooked.

Makes about 6 cups; serves 12 • Prep Time: 15 minutes • Cook Time: 3 hours

¼ cup **olive oil**

2 large **onions**, chopped

4 large cloves **garlic**, finely chopped

2 (28-ounce) cans whole Italian plum **tomatoes**, chopped

1 (28-ounce) can **tomato puree**

2 cups dry **red wine**

1 cup water

1 teaspoon dried **basil**

Salt and freshly ground black pepper

1 Heat the oil in a large pot over medium-high heat. Sauté the onions and garlic for about 4 minutes, until transparent. Add the tomatoes, tomato paste, wine, water, and basil and bring to a boil. Reduce the heat, cover, and simmer for 3 hours. During the last hour, partially uncover the pot and let the sauce cook down until thickened. Season to taste.

2 For leftover sauce, let cool to room temperature. Place 2 cups of sauce in a freezer bag, mark and date the bag, and freeze for up to 3 months. To use again, let thaw, then warm in a saucepan.

3 Slow Cooker Method: Transfer the sautéed onions and garlic to a large-capacity slow cooker, and add the remaining ingredients, but omit the water. Cover and cook on Low for 6 to 8 hours, until the flavors have combined and the sauce has thickened.

Calories 50 • Total Fat 2g • Saturated Fat 0g • Carbohydrates 4g
Protein 0.5g • Dietary Fiber 1g • Sodium 5mg

Adventure helps us learn new things, and stay active and engaged in the world. Isolation is not good for anyone, and adventure and interest encourage our growing from interacting with others.

~Jane Murray, MD, Sastun Center of Integrative Health Care

Veggie Burger with Roasted Tomato, Garlic, and Basil Topping

When you find a veggie burger (usually soy-based) that you like—especially one made locally—buy a bunch and keep them in your freezer. Likewise, make a batch of Roasted Tomato, Garlic, and Basil Topping, enjoy some, then freeze the rest in small containers. When you need a quick meal, simply cook the burger according to package directions, thaw and reheat the topping, and you're in burger heaven.

Serves 4 • Prep Time: 5 minutes • Cook Time: 15 minutes

4 veggie burgers, cooked according to package directions

1 cup prepared **Roasted Tomato**, **Garlic**, and **Basil** Topping (page 103)

1 cup shredded romaine

4 whole wheat buns, sliced in half and toasted

1 Place each cooked veggie burger on a bottom bun, then top with ¼ cup each of the topping and the lettuce. Place the top bun over romaine and serve.

Calories 248 • Total Fat 7g • Saturated Fat 2g • Carbohydrates 15g Protein 29g • Dietary Fiber 2.5g • Sodium 242mg

Feel-Good Lasagne

If you want to make your own lasagne but think it's too hard to figure out how to make one that is good for you, go for this one. It has all the flavors, layers, and textures of traditional lasagne, but with the added benefit of good-for-you foods and a "less fat is more" philosophy. This recipe is based on one served at the famous Canyon Ranch spas. The recipe looks long, but it assembles fast. Put it in two 8-inch square pans so you can freeze one and enjoy one today.

Serves 8 • Prep Time: 25 minutes • Cook Time: 60 minutes

BOLOGNESE SAUCE

1½ teaspoons **olive oil**

12 ounces ground **turkey** or vegetarian Italian sausage meat, bulk or removed from its casings

1 cup chopped **onion**

1 tablespoon minced **garlic**

2 teaspoons dried **basil**

1 teaspoon dried **oregano**

2 cups **Slow-Simmered Tomato Sauce with Red Wine** (page 206) or your favorite marinara sauce

RICOTTA FILLING

2 cups fat-free ricotta cheese

2 **egg** yolks, beaten

1 teaspoon dried **basil**

½ teaspoon dried **oregano**

½ teaspoon salt

¼ teaspoon ground black pepper

3 cups **Slow-Simmered Tomato Sauce with Red Wine** (page 206) or your favorite marinara sauce

9 ounces whole wheat lasagne noodles, no-boil or boiled according to package directions

¾ cup freshly grated **Parmesan** cheese

¾ cup shredded mozzarella cheese

1 Coat a 9 by 13-inch baking dish with a small amount of butter or oil and set aside.

2 For the Bolognese sauce, heat the oil in a skillet over medium-high heat. Sauté the turkey sausage, onion, and garlic for about 7 minutes, until the sausage is cooked through and the onion has softened. Stir in the basil, oregano, and tomato sauce. Remove from the heat.

3 For the filling, stir the ricotta, egg yolks, basil, oregano, salt, and pepper together in a bowl until well blended.

4 To assemble, smooth 1 cup of the tomato sauce in the bottom of the pan and top with one-fourth of the noodles. Top with half of the filling and spread evenly with a knife or spatula. Top with 1 cup of the Bolognese sauce and sprinkle with ¼ cup of the Parmesan. Layer another one-fourth of the noodles, topping them with ½ cup of the tomato sauce, 1 cup of the Bolognese sauce, and ¼ cup of the mozzarella. Layer the remaining noodles and spread with the remaining filling. Top with the remaining Bolognese and tomato sauces, then the remaining cheeses. Cover with aluminum foil and bake right away, refrigerate for up to 24 hours before baking, or freeze.

5 To bake, preheat the oven to 350°F. Bake, covered, for 45 to 50 minutes, or until bubbling. Let cool in the pan for 15 minutes before slicing and serving. To bake when frozen, let the lasagne sit at room temperature for 30 minutes while the oven preheats. Bake, covered, for 80 to 90 minutes, or until bubbling.

Calories 329 • Total Fat 12.5g • Saturated Fat 5g • Carbohydrates 24.5g
Protein 27g • Dietary Fiber 1.3g • Sodium 425mg

Pan-Seared Chicken Breasts with Artichoke Sun-Dried Tomato Pesto and Asparagus

The secret to a perfectly—and quickly—cooked chicken breast is to cut it down to size. Simply place a boneless, skinless chicken breast flat on a cutting board and, holding a sharp knife parallel to the board, cut in half lengthwise, so the chicken breast is half as thick as it was. It helps to first put the chicken breast in the freezer for 30 minutes. Once you have this technique down, you can cook chicken breasts in about 10 minutes on your stovetop in a skillet, grill pan, or griddle. Chicken breasts cooked this way are also delicious served atop baby spinach (so it wilts) or with steamed asparagus, then drizzled with a tablespoon of Work of Art Drizzle (page 145). Leftovers taste great for lunch the next day over greens or in a sandwich. And any leftover pesto is delicious served on slices of Whole Wheat and Flaxseed Boule (page 120). If you like, make the pesto a day ahead and keep it in the refrigerator.

Serves 4 • Prep Time: 15 minutes • Cook Time: 45 minutes

ARTICHOKE SUN-DRIED TOMATO PESTO

½ cup canned or thawed frozen **artichokes**, chopped

4 cloves **garlic**, minced

½ cup dry-packed sun-dried **tomatoes**

¼ cup finely chopped **green onions**, with some green

¼ cup grated **Parmesan cheese**

½ teaspoon dried **oregano**

1 tablespoon fresh **lemon juice**

¼ cup hot water

2 teaspoons **olive oil**

Salt and pepper

4 (4-ounce) boneless, skinless **chicken breasts**, halved lengthwise (see headnote above)

1 pound thin **asparagus** spears, tough ends trimmed, cut diagonally into 2-inch pieces

continued on next page

1   Preheat the oven to 400°F.

2   For the pesto, arrange the artichokes on a rimmed baking sheet lined with parchment paper and coat with a small amount of oil or butter. Roast for 20 to 25 minutes, until lightly browned. Transfer the artichokes to a food processor or blender. Add the garlic, sun-dried tomatoes, green onions, cheese, oregano, and lemon juice. Blend until very finely chopped. Blend in the water, 1 tablespoon at a time, until the pesto is smoother and spreadable.

3   Heat the oil in a large skillet over medium-high heat. Season the chicken breasts on both sides. Sauté the chicken for 3 to 5 minutes, until browned on both sides, and keep warm on a plate. Add the asparagus to the pan and cook, turning occasionally, for 5 minutes, or until the asparagus is crisp-tender. Portion the chicken breasts on four plates, top with the pesto, and serve the asparagus on the side.

Calories 249 • Total Fat 8g • Saturated Fat 2.5g • Carbohydrates 12.5g
Protein 32g • Dietary Fiber 5g • Sodium 317mg

Your largest organ needs your TLC!

By Betsy Medina, of Indigo Wild®

Believe it or not, what you put on your body is just as important as what you put in your body. Why? Because your skin is your largest organ; what you put on it is absorbed by your entire body. Using products made with natural ingredients and scented with pure essential oils is the best way to care for your skin. Look for products scented with pure essential oils, rather than synthetic fragrance oils. Fragrance oils can cause headaches and skin irritation. Pure essential oils are natural plant extracts, and when used in high concentrations, they are aromatherapeutic. Different essential oils affect the mind and body in different ways. For example, lavender is widely used as a remedy for headaches, stress, and insomnia, while rosemary promotes alertness and helps with memory.

Here are 10 fun and easy ways to use essential oils in your daily life:

1. Apply lavender or tea tree oil to cuts, scrapes, or scratches.

2. Place a few drops onto a radiator scent ring to fill a room with aromatherapy.

3. Drop a couple of drops of your favorite essential oil onto padded hangers to keep closets and clothes smelling fresh.

4. Place a drop of lemon oil on a soft cloth to polish your copper.

5. Place 1 to 2 drops of rosemary on your hairbrush to promote hair growth and thickness.

6. Add a few drops of thyme to your diffuser when the flu is going around.

7. Place a few drops of your favorite oil onto a piece of terry cloth and toss in with your clothes in the dryer.

8. Add a few drops of your favorite essential oil into a water spray bottle for a natural and aromatherapeutic air freshener.

9. Add a few drops of your favorite essential oil into vegetable oil and use as a massage oil for sore muscles.

10. Place a few drops of geranium essential oil into your shoes to freshen them up.

Lemony Chicken and Mushroom Stir-Fry with Quinoa

In a wok—or a large skillet—you can stir up this dish in 40 minutes, which makes it the answer when you're up for flavor and low-fat fare. For quick work of the ginger, use a fine-rasp grater; microplane is a popular brand. You can substitute turkey breast, shrimp, or vegetable protein, such as soy, for the chicken. And replace the quinoa with brown rice or couscous to suit your taste.

Serves 4 • Prep Time: 15 minutes • Cook Time: 35 minutes

2 teaspoons grated **lemon zest**

3 tablespoons fresh **lemon juice**

2 tablespoons **soy sauce**

2 tablespoons dry sherry or chicken broth

2 tablespoons grated fresh **ginger** (see page 77)

1 teaspoon sugar

1 tablespoon water

2 teaspoons cornstarch

8 ounces boneless, skinless **chicken breasts**, cut crosswise into ½-inch strips

   Salt and ¼ teaspoon freshly ground black pepper

1 cup **quinoa**

1½ cups water

2 teaspoons **grapeseed or olive oil**

8 ounces fresh **mushrooms**, thinly sliced

½ large red **bell pepper**, seeded and thinly sliced

2 large cloves **garlic**, minced

6 ounces baby **spinach**

1 Whisk the lemon zest, lemon juice, soy sauce, sherry, ginger, and sugar together in a bowl. Whisk in the water and cornstarch until the cornstarch dissolves. Sprinkle the chicken strips with pepper and add them to the marinade.

2 Rinse the quinoa twice to remove the soapy natural coating. Bring the water to a boil in a medium saucepan over medium-high heat. Stir in the quinoa, cover, and reduce the heat to medium-low. Cook for 15 to 20 minutes, until the quinoa has popped open and is tender. Fluff with a fork, season with salt and pepper, and keep warm.

3 Heat a wok or large skillet over medium-high heat for 3 minutes. Add the oil and tilt to coat. Remove the chicken from the marinade, reserving the marinade, and stir-fry for 2 minutes. Add the mushrooms, bell pepper, and garlic and stir-fry for about 3 minutes, until the mushrooms are browned at the edges. Add the remaining marinade and cook , stirring, for about 1½ minutes, until the sauce is reduced to a glaze. Mix in the spinach.

4 To serve, portion the quinoa onto plates and top with the stir-fry mixture.

Calories 157 • Total Fat 4.5g • Saturated Fat 1g • Carbohydrates 11g
Protein 16.5g • Dietary Fiber 2g • Sodium 377mg

Gardening as Therapy for Body and Soul

In the August 2003 *Cancer Nursing*, it was reported that researchers at the University of Michigan School of Nursing found that participating in activities that involve nature improved the ability to think clearly, keep track, set goals, and start a task and follow it through—in a study of women treated for breast cancer. According to researchers, the restorative effects of communing with nature may be partially due to the feelings of respite they induce.

"These activities aren't the kind that hit you over the head," said Bernadine Cimprich, an associate professor of nursing at the University of Michigan School of Nursing and the study's lead author. "They give you enough room to reflect on things, to ponder your values and priorities. They move you away from daily demands and pressures."

According to Dr. Max Wicha, director of the University of Michigan Comprehensive Cancer Center, "In pioneering research [Cimprich], has come up with some very important observations on how breast cancer patients' lives can be changed for the better through interactions with the natural environment." As we all know, wearing gardening gloves and protective clothing makes gardening fun and cuts down on the knicks and scrapes, and reduces the risk of lymphedema, as well.

Turkey, Apple, and Cranberry Wrap

This yummy wrap sandwich has lots of good things going for it, not the least being that it's a meal in itself, with protein, carbs, veggies, and fruit. If you like, use cooked chicken, tofu, or falafel (garbanzo bean patty) in place of the turkey.

Serves 6 • Prep Time: 15 minutes

8 ounces cooked **turkey breast**, finely chopped or shredded, or **vegetable protein patty**, such as falafel

2 tablespoons minced **red onion**

¼ cup chopped **apple**

¼ cup seedless **red grapes**, cut in half

2 tablespoons dried **cranberries**, snipped with kitchen shears into smaller pieces

2 tablespoons **olive oil** mayonnaise

2 tablespoons nonfat **Greek yogurt**, such as Fage

1 tablespoon 2% **milk** or skim milk

1 clove **garlic**, minced

1 tablespoon Dijon mustard

Salt and pepper

6 (10-inch) whole wheat tortillas

1½ cups baby **spinach**

1 For the filling, combine the turkey, onion, apple, grapes, and cranberries in a bowl.

2 For the dressing, whisk the mayonnaise, yogurt, milk, garlic, and mustard together in a bowl. Spoon over the filling and stir to blend. Season to taste.

3 To assemble, place each tortilla on a flat surface. Arrange ¼ cup of the spinach on each tortilla. Top with ¼ cup of the filling. Roll up tightly, burrito style. Serve right away or cover and refrigerate for up to 24 hours.

Calories 170 • Total Fat 3g • Saturated Fat 0.5g • Carbohydrates 24g
Protein 13g • Dietary Fiber 3.5g • Sodium 310mg

Festive Cider-Glazed Turkey Breast with Roasted Sweet Potatoes

Who says that a memorable meal has to just be saved for official holidays? Change the apple juice to something else to make a flavor change—perhaps orange juice. For a weekend or holiday dinner, this dish is one that does you good and pleases friends and family.

Serves 6 • Prep Time: 25 minutes • Cook Time: 1 hour and 15 minutes

1   (1½ to 2 pounds) boneless **turkey breast**

3   large **sweet potatoes**, diced

1   large **red onion**, diced

1   tablespoon fresh **rosemary** leaves

1   tablespoon **olive oil** or **canola oil**

    Salt and pepper

½   cup **apple juice** or **apple cider**

2   tablespoons **honey**

    Fresh rosemary sprigs, for garnish

1   Preheat the oven to 350°F.

2   Rinse the turkey and pat dry. Place the turkey, skin side up, in a shallow roasting pan. In a large bowl, combine the sweet potatoes, onion, and rosemary. Drizzle with 2 teaspoons of the oil, season with salt and pepper, and toss to blend. Scatter around the turkey. Brush the turkey with the remaining oil and season with salt and pepper. Insert a meat thermometer into the thickest part of the turkey breast, not touching a bone.

3   Roast for 30 minutes, then stir the vegetables. Return to the oven and roast for 20 minutes longer.

4   In a small saucepan over medium-high heat, whisk the apple juice and honey together until the honey dissolves into the juice and bubbles form around the perimeter of the pan. Spoon half the glaze over the turkey and vegetables and roast for about 15 minutes longer, until the turkey reaches an internal temperature of 170°F and the sweet potatoes are tender and browned.

5 To serve, transfer the turkey to a cutting board and let rest for 10 to 15 minutes. Carve into thin slices. Serve over the sweet potato mixture and drizzle with the remaining glaze. Garnish with rosemary sprigs.

Calories 275 • Total Fat 3g • Saturated Fat 0.5g • Carbohydrates 31.5g
Protein 29g • Dietary Fiber 3g • Sodium 84mg

WHO KNEW?

Q: How do I know if my doggie bag or leftover food is safe to eat?

A: Putting leftover food in the refrigerator or freezer typically stops bacteria in their tracks. According to the March 2010 issue of the *Nutrition Action Healthletter* from the Center for Science in the Public Interest (CSPI), "with enough warmth, moisture and nutrients, one bacterium that divides every half-hour can produce 17 million progeny in 12 hours." Toss out the "leftover" leftovers following these specific rules for leftovers from CSPI and the USDA:

2 hours—2 inches—4 days:

- 2 hours from oven to refrigerator or freezer, or throw it out

- 2 inches thick to cool quickly in a shallow pan, in order to speed up chilling

- 4 days in the refrigerator or freeze it

Power Pilaf

When you want a quick whole-grain side dish that cooks in minutes, simply add 1 cup of this mixture to 2 cups boiling water, broth, or almond milk. You can find larger "beads" of Israeli couscous, tiny chopped dried garbanzo beans, very tiny brown quinoa, and tear-shaped orzo pasta in the bulk aisle of the grocery or health food store. Use a clean coffee grinder or a food processor to finely chop the dried garbanzo beans. Trader Joe's multicolored Harvest Grains blend is a delicious, convenient store-bought option. Note: If you like, stir 1 tablespoon or so of ground flaxseed into the pilaf before serving. Keep ground flaxseed, covered, in the freezer and just take out what you need.

Makes 2 cups; serves 4 • Prep Time: 5 minutes • Cook Time: 15 minutes

1   cup Israeli or pearl couscous

⅓   cup finely chopped dried **garbanzo beans**

⅓   cup **quinoa**

⅓   cup orzo pasta

2   cups water, broth, **almond milk**, rice milk, or skim milk

1 Combine the couscous, garbanzo beans, quinoa, and orzo. Store the mixture in an airtight container and keep in a cool, dry place.

2 To prepare, scoop out 1 cup of the dry pilaf mix. Bring the liquid to a boil. Add the dry mixture, reduce the heat, cover, and simmer for 8 to 10 minutes, until tender. Fluff with a fork.

Calories 90 • Total Fat 0.5g • Saturated Fat 0g • Carbohydrates 15g
Protein 3g • Dietary Fiber 1.5g • Sodium 0mg

Burgundy Beef with Fresh Mushrooms, Herbs, and Noodles

It's always great to have a slow-cooking, great-tasting entrée in your repertoire. Grass-fed lean beef, in moderation, has lots of good things going for it besides flavor—protein and zinc, for instance. Combine it with a little red wine, onion, and mushrooms, and you've got a fabulous dish with a French flair. Steam some thin French green beans (haricots verts), found in the produce department or frozen food section, to go with it. Serve leftover beef au jus, thinly sliced, with Whole Wheat and Flaxseed Baguettes (page 119) for a French dip sandwich.

Serves 6 • Prep Time: 30 minutes • Cook Time: 6 to 10 hours

1 large **onion**, thinly sliced

1 (2½-pound) **beef brisket** or **bottom round roast**, trimmed of fat

2 cloves **garlic**, minced

1 teaspoon dried **oregano** or thyme

½ teaspoon ground black pepper

1 cup dry **red wine** or low-sodium beef broth

¾ cup low-sodium beef broth

1 tablespoon Worcestershire sauce

2 large **carrots**, cut into 1-inch pieces

8 ounces **mushrooms**, sliced

1 pound egg noodles, cooked according to package directions

Steamed whole thin green beans

Fresh **oregano** or thyme sprigs, for garnish

1 Arrange the onion in the bottom of a 3½ to 5-quart slow cooker. Place the beef on top of the onion and season with the garlic, oregano, and pepper. (If necessary, cut the beef into pieces to fit into your slow cooker.) Pour the wine, broth, and Worcestershire sauce around the beef. Cover and cook on the Low setting for 9 to 10 hours for brisket, 6 to 7 hours for bottom round, or in a large roasting or baking dish, covered, in a 250°F oven for the same length of time, adding water as necessary, until the beef is fork-tender.

2 About 1 hour before the beef is ready, add the carrots and mushrooms, cover, and continue cooking on Low, or until the carrots are tender.

3 To serve, remove the beef and slice very thinly or shred. Transfer the vegetables with a slotted spoon to a bowl and keep warm. Strain any fat from the jus. Serve the beef over the noodles and top with the carrots and mushrooms and a spoonful of jus. Serve the green beans on the side. Garnish with a sprig of oregano and serve.

Calories 200 • Total Fat 6g • Saturated Fat 1g
Carbohydrates 30g • Protein 25g • Dietary Fiber 2g
Sodium 45mg

TREAT OF THE DAY

Knit to your heart's content!

More than to simply have something warm to wrap around their neck on a cold winter day, needlepointers, knitters, and crocheters have another reason to keep on stitching: New studies show that knitting, crocheting, and similar repetitive needlework provide a number of health benefits. Rhythmic, repetitive acts help to manage stress, pain, and depression, which in turn strengthen the body's immune system and are a good form of distraction.

Physiotherapists are suggesting that the act of knitting actually changes brain chemistry, decreasing stress hormones and increasing feel-good serotonin and dopamine.

Some doctors also suggest that the repetitive movements of knitting affect the same areas in the brain as meditation and yoga, which have been shown to help prevent pain and depression and relieve stress and increase relaxation.

Note: Be kind to your hands and arms and don't over-do it to avoid lymphedema.

Highway 1 Meatloaf
with Power Pilaf and Baby Greens

One bite of our meatloaf takes you to your favorite place, down your favorite road, in your favorite frame of mind. Made with ground turkey, roasted red pepper, and Parmesan, this meatloaf has all the flavor and texture of one made with beef. Make sure that you save some for a cold meatloaf sandwich for the next day. Instead of offering a more traditional side dish of mashed potatoes, serve this with cooked Power Pilaf and fresh salad greens. Top everything with Roasted Tomato Sauce.

Serves 8 • Prep Time: 25 minutes • Cook Time: 45 minutes

1½ pounds ground **turkey**

½ cup finely chopped **onion**

½ cup unseasoned or Panko bread crumbs

1 teaspoon dried **oregano**

1 large **egg**, beaten

¾ cup grated **Romano**, **Parmesan**, or **Asiago cheese**

2 tablespoons Dijon mustard

1 cup finely chopped fresh Italian **parsley**

1 (7-ounce) jar roasted **red peppers**, drained and rinsed, finely chopped

Salt and pepper

ROASTED TOMATO SAUCE

8 Roma **tomatoes**, cut in half lengthwise

¼ cup Work of Art Drizzle (page 145)

2 cups cooked **Power Pilaf** (page 221)

8 cups baby **greens**

1 Preheat the oven to 400°F. Coat a 7 by 11-inch baking dish with a small amount of oil or butter. Line a rimmed baking sheet with aluminum foil.

2 For the meatloaf, combine the turkey, onion, bread crumbs, oregano, egg, cheese, mustard, parsley, and roasted red peppers in a large bowl. Season with salt and pepper and mix until well combined. Form the mixture into a 9-inch loaf in the prepared baking dish.

3 For the Roasted Tomato Sauce, place the tomatoes cut side down on the prepared baking sheet.

4   Place the meatloaf on the top shelf and the tomatoes on the bottom shelf of the oven. Bake for 15 minutes, then transfer the tomatoes to a wire rack to cool. Continue baking the meatloaf for 30 minutes longer, or until an instant-read thermometer inserted in the center registers 165°F. Let rest for 15 minutes before slicing.

5   To finish the sauce, peel, seed, and finely chop the roasted tomatoes and combine with the Work of Art Drizzle.

6   To serve, cut the meatloaf into 8 slices. Serve a slice of meatloaf, a spoonful of pilaf, and 1 cup greens on each plate. Spoon over all with a little sauce and serve.

Calories 243 • Total Fat 12g • Saturated Fat 4g • Carbohydrates 8.5g
Protein 23g • Dietary Fiber 1g • Sodium 350mg

Gardening does a body good.

Tending to a garden can be a great form of exercise. According to Melicia Whitt, PhD, an epidemiologist at the University of Pennsylvania School of Medicine, gardening can—depending on the task—provide as much of a workout as sports such as kayaking and weight lifting. Gardening burns calories: Approximately 125 calories are burned after just 30 minutes of gardening. Plus, your garden can be a source of the healthy vegetables used in these recipes. Remember, as with any physical activity, don't overdo it. Talk to your doctor if you experience any pain or discomfort.

ON THE UPSWING

It's important to take time each day to listen to yourself and what you need. There are many who will give you advice, and you will see other survivors approaching their recovery in different ways. But it is important to know that you are unique.

~Carol LaRue, author and occupational therapist

Barbecue Sirloin Steak Strips with Smoky Peppers and Polenta

Hearty, smoky, colorful, and satisfying, this quick-cook dish is a crowd pleaser. Everyone seems to love small pieces of meat in fabulous sauce—and you cannot argue with the quick preparation. No fuss, but lots of flavor. Any leftovers can be packed up for lunch.

Serves 4 • Prep Time: 5 minutes • Cook Time: 20 minutes

STEAK AND PEPPERS

1 tablespoon **olive oil**

1½ pounds boneless **sirloin steak**, trimmed of fat and cut into 1-inch strips

1 large **onion**, thinly sliced

1 (12-ounce) jar **roasted red** and/ or **yellow peppers**, coarsely chopped

½ cup hickory- or mesquite-flavored **tomato-based barbecue sauce** (such as KC Masterpiece)

POLENTA

2 cups 2% **milk**

2 cups water

1 cup quick-cooking polenta or yellow cornmeal

Salt and pepper

¼ cup chopped fresh Italian **parsley**

1 For the steak and peppers, heat the oil in a large skillet over medium-high heat. Add the steak strips and cook, stirring, for 4 minutes, or until the desired doneness. Transfer to a plate to keep warm. Add the onion and cook, stirring, for about 4 minutes, until the onion has softened. Stir in the roasted peppers and barbecue sauce and stir to blend. Simmer for 10 minutes, or until the sauce has slightly thickened. Remove from the heat and add the steak back to the pan.

2 For the polenta, bring the milk and water to a boil in a large saucepan over high heat. Whisk in the polenta and cook, whisking, for about 2 minutes, until the polenta thickens. Remove from the heat and season with salt and pepper.

3 To serve, spoon the polenta on each plate, top with the steak and pepper mixture, and garnish with the parsley.

Calories 120 • Total Fat 5g • Saturated Fat 1g • Carbohydrates 12g
Protein 15g • Dietary Fiber 3g • Sodium 250mg

Shrimp Fra Diavolo

Adapted from a recipe by acclaimed chef and cookbook author Lidia Bastianich, this version is a little leaner but still delicious. Serve a cup of spinach on each plate; then pile on the shrimp, beautifully wilting the lovely bed of spinach; finally, accompany with Whole Wheat and Flaxseed Baguettes (page 119) for an easy meal. For a heartier dish, serve with whole wheat linguini or spaghetti . . . and for a vegetarian or vegan option, use tofu or other vegetable protein in place of the shrimp.

Serves 4 • Prep Time: 5 minutes • Cook Time: 15 minutes

3 tablespoons **olive oil**

4 cloves **garlic**, minced

2 pounds jumbo **shrimp**, peeled and deveined

Salt and pepper

2 (16-ounce) cans Italian plum **tomatoes**, chopped, with juice

½ teaspoon **red pepper flakes**

½ cup or one handful fresh **basil** leaves, torn

4 cups baby **spinach**

2 tablespoons chopped fresh Italian **parsley**, for garnish

1 Heat the oil in a large skillet over medium-high heat. Sauté the garlic about 1 minute, until golden. Add the shrimp in a single layer and cook, turning once, for about 3 minutes, until lightly golden and opaque. Sprinkle with salt and pepper. With a slotted spoon, transfer the shrimp to a plate to keep warm.

2 Stir the tomatoes into the pan and cook, stirring, for 5 minutes. Stir in the red pepper flakes and continue to cook for about 5 minutes longer, until the sauce is lightly thickened.

3 Stir in the shrimp and basil and cook for about 1 minute, until the shrimp are heated through. To serve, place 1 cup of spinach on each plate. Top with one-fourth of the shrimp mixture, and garnish each serving with parsley.

Calories 140 • Total Fat 6g • Saturated Fat 1g • Carbohydrates 3g
Protein 15g • Dietary Fiber 1g • Sodium 200mg

Acupuncture may ease joint pain associated with some breast cancer treatments.

Researchers at New York-Presbyterian Hospital/Columbia University Medical Center have found that acupuncture is effective in reducing joint pain and stiffness in breast cancer patients who are being treated with commonly used hormonal therapies.

In a study report released on August 23, 2010, by the medical center, forty-three women receiving an aromatase inhibitor for early breast cancer received either true acupuncture or a "pretend" acupuncture twice a week for six weeks. All had also reported musculoskeletal pain.

The participants being treated with true acupuncture experienced a significant improvement in joint pain and stiffness over the course of the study. In addition, 20 percent of the patients who had reported taking pain relief medications reported that they no longer needed to take these medications following acupuncture treatment. Participants who received the pretend acupuncture did not report improvements in their pain.

"This study suggests that acupuncture may help women manage the joint pain and stiffness that can accompany aromatase inhibitor treatment," said the study's lead author, Dr. Katherine Crew.

Studies show that acupuncture may:

Help relieve fatigue

Control hot flashes

Help decrease nausea

Reduce vomiting

Lessen pain

In acupuncture, sterile, hair-thin needles are inserted into specific points on the skin, called "acupuncture points," and then gently moved. Researchers propose that acupuncture stimulates the nervous system to release natural painkillers and immune system cells, which then travel to weakened areas of the body and relieve symptoms.

Note: Anyone who has had lymph nodes removed from under an arm should not have needles inserted into that arm. If acupuncture is used on the arm, there is a risk of lymphedema, swelling caused by an excess of fluid in the arm. Talk to the acupuncturist about other treatments that could be used on that arm, such as aromatherapy.

Provençal Salmon Aioli Platter

The beauty of this dish is in its presentation, flavor, and adaptability. Although the aioli platter is traditional in the south of France during the winter, it's delicious in any season—whether served hot, cold, or at room temperature. In addition to the artichokes and steamed new potatoes, simply choose two seasonal vegetables for the platter, and you've got it. To treat yourself without overdoing it, just dollop about 1 tablespoon of the wonderful garlicky mayonnaise on your plate—believe us, that's plenty—and enjoy. This dish works well for buffet or family-style entertaining. Everyone just helps themselves to a bit of salmon, some vegetables, and a spoonful of aioli. Plan on 4 ounces of salmon and 1 tablespoon of aioli per serving. The leftover aioli will keep for 7 to 10 days, covered, in the refrigerator.

To make this dish vegetarian or vegan, use a mound of cooked white or garbanzo beans, glistened with a little olive oil and spikes of fresh rosemary leaves, in place of the salmon.

Serves 8 • Prep Time: 15 minutes • Cook Time: 25 minutes

AIOLI

1 cup good-quality **olive oil** mayonnaise

2 teaspoons grated **lemon zest**

2 tablespoons fresh **lemon juice**

2 cloves **garlic**, minced

Fine kosher or sea salt

1 (2-pound) skinless **salmon** fillet

1 teaspoon **olive oil**

Kosher salt and freshly ground black pepper

9 ounces thawed frozen **artichoke** hearts

2 pounds small new potatoes, cooked until tender

1 pound cherry **tomatoes**, raw **zucchini**, and/or yellow **summer squash**, cut into spears or coins

1 pound **asparagus**, green beans, or baby **carrots**, steamed

continued on next page

ON THE UPSWING

Think of your visit to a hair salon as getting a work of art done on your "living canvas." What a wonderful gift to give yourself and for your stylist to give to you—beautiful art that lives and breathes!

~Vilma Subel, owner, Xiphium Salon

1   Preheat the oven to 425°F. Line a large rimmed baking sheet with parchment paper.

2   For the aioli, whisk the mayonnaise, lemon zest, lemon juice, and garlic together in a medium bowl. Season to taste.

3   Rinse the salmon, pat dry, and place skin side down on the prepared pan. Brush with olive oil and season with salt and pepper. Roast for 20 to 22 minutes, until the salmon begins to flake when tested with a fork in the thickest part. Serve hot or cover and refrigerate, then let come to room temperature until ready to serve.

4   To serve, arrange the salmon in the center of a large platter. Arrange the artichokes, potatoes, tomatoes, and asparagus around the salmon. Place the aioli in a small bowl with a serving spoon.

TIP: All fish fillets have a skin side—where the skin was removed. The flesh is usually a little discolored or gray from the skin.

Calories 150 • Total Fat 9g • Saturated Fat 1.5g • Carbohydrates 15g
Protein 12g • Dietary Fiber 3g • Sodium 150mg

WOULD SOMEONE JUST TELL ME . . .

Q: Why doesn't anyone talk about how stressful it is when treatment is over? Feeling as if I am not doing something to prevent cancer anymore is driving me crazy.

A: First, identify your emotions. This can be more difficult than you might think, so it is going to take some practice. Try sitting in a quiet place and closing your eyes. Notice what is going on inside your body. Is your heart racing; do you feel a ball in the pit of your stomach; are your shoulders tense? What is making you feel this way? Try keeping a log, writing down your emotions and labeling them.

Now that you have identified your emotions and their effect on your body, sit with them. Let them be. Do not judge the emotions. Emotions (like food) are not good or bad. They just are. A therapist once told me that "emotions are a message from your soul." Instead of pushing the emotions away, embrace them and let your body process them.

Try these exercises that research has shown can help train your brain to think more positively. By reflecting on positive memories or emotions, you can use the suggestions below as distraction techniques to push away the negative thoughts and soothe yourself.

Simple Tips for Getting Yourself "Unstuck":

- Close your eyes and imagine a positive experience. Recall how that experience felt and embrace those feelings. Allow yourself to smile. Take a big inhale and seal in those positive thoughts, then exhale completely. Open your eyes and enjoy the positive energy you just generated.

- When you get stuck and cannot move forward, ask for help—from a friend, family member, or health care professional, who understands you and supports you unconditionally.

- Be your own cheerleader. Take a stack of your favorite colored sticky notes (check out the rainbow-colored stack) and write positive statements on them. Stick them in spots that you look at throughout the day—on your bathroom mirror, your computer monitor, your refrigerator, in your car.

- Make a list of things you love about living, and try to do at least one of those things every day so you have something positive to look forward to. Cultivate positivity like a garden in your life!

When It Comes to Your Heart . . .

Certain breast cancer treatments, chest radiation, deficiency of exercise during treatments, and stress, have been found to make women more susceptible to heart disease.

"Most breast cancer therapies today—including new treatments still under development—increase long-term risk of cardiovascular disease," says Lee W. Jones, PhD, an exercise physiologist and associate professor in the Department of Surgery at Duke University Medical Center, Durham, North Carolina. "We don't know exactly how large the added risk is, but we believe it's substantial. Recent gains in breast cancer specific survival could be markedly diminished by an increase in the long-term risk of cardiovascular death."

Pamela S. Douglas, MD, chief of cardiology at Duke University and coauthor of an article in the October 2007 *Journal of the American College of Cardiology*, said although the damage comes from chemotherapy, "the benefit of saving lives outweighed the risks and were just part inside the accepted cost" of the treatment. But with the success of treatment and developing survivor numbers, Douglas and her colleagues are urging physicians to take the long view when determining a woman's breast cancer treatment. First, deal with the cancer, but don't forget about cardiovascular health down the road.

Talk with your health care provider about whether your "treatment after primary treatment" care plan should include a cardiology follow-up. In addition, long-term use of aromatase inhibitors, drugs often prescribed for breast cancer patients, may increase the risk of heart problems for postmenopausal women, according to a Canadian researcher (see page 153). If you are taking an aromatase inhibitor, talk with your physician about adding a cardiology component to your annual checkup. Clearly, cancer treatment consists of the right combination of medicine and living a healthy lifestyle.

Seared Tuna with Baby Bok Choy, Black Pearl Rice, and Fresh Ginger Vinaigrette

This recipe title almost takes longer to say than the recipe does to make. Vivid with color, flavor, and texture, this is a great way to eat well and enjoy yourself, too. You simply sear the tuna in a hot skillet for a few minutes on each side, then serve it sliced and rare. Black pearl rice has lots of extra antioxidants and a flavor similar to, but milder than, wild rice. You can find it at better grocery stores in bulk or packaged by Annie Chun. You will need to cook 2 cups black rice in salted water to get 4 cups cooked for this recipe.

Serves 4 • Prep Time: 5 minutes • Cook Time: 15 minutes

1 cup Fresh Ginger Vinaigrette (page 155)

8 baby **bok choy**, trimmed and quartered, or 1 pound **Brussels sprouts**, trimmed and quartered

¼ cup water

4 (6-ounce) yellowfin or ahi **tuna steaks**, 1 inch thick, rinsed and patted dry

1 tablespoon **grapeseed oil** or **canola oil**

Salt and pepper

4 cups cooked black pearl **rice**

1 Drizzle ¼ cup of the vinaigrette over the bok choy in a large nonstick skillet with a lid. Add the water and bring to a boil over medium-high heat. Cook, covered, stirring occasionally, for about 8 minutes, until the bok choy is crisp-tender. Keep warm.

2 Heat a cast-iron or other heavy skillet or griddle over medium-high heat until hot. Brush both sides of the tuna with oil and season with salt and pepper. Sear the tuna for about 2 minutes on each side, turning once, until rare. Remove from the heat and let the tuna rest for 5 minutes before slicing.

3 To serve, place 1 cup of the rice on each plate. Top with the tuna slices and baby bok choy. Drizzle with the remaining vinaigrette and serve.

TIP: For a vegetarian or vegan dish, use vegetable broth in the Ginger Vinaigrette. Use half of it to marinate vegetable protein, then sear it as for the tuna. Assemble the dish as above.

Calories 250 • Total Fat 2g • Saturated Fat 0g • Carbohydrates 30g
Protein 15g • Dietary Fiber 1g • Sodium 60mg

Scientific Reasons to Watch a Funny Movie

Even anticipating a humorous experience can enhance our health. In April 7, 2008, the American Physiological Society published findings of researchers at Loma Linda University who studied a group of sixteen healthy male volunteers. The participants were assigned to two groups. Blood was drawn from both groups four times during the event and three times afterward. The experimental group was told that they would be watching a humorous video, while the control group was not.

The findings were astounding. The experimental group showed not only a decrease in stress hormones (cortisol, epinephrine, and dopac) but also an increase in beta-endorphins (chemicals that alleviate depression) and human growth hormone (which boosts immunity).

According to Dr. Lee Berk, the team's lead researcher: "Our findings lead us to believe that by seeking out positive experiences that make us laugh, we can do a lot with our physiology to stay well." In an earlier study, Dr. Berk's experimental group watched a humorous video. Blood samples were measured on both the experimental group (that watched the humorous video) and a control group (that did not watch the video). The results revealed positive biochemical changes for the experimental group who watched the funny video. In addition, Dr. Berk measured the positive physiological changes that occur after a session of laughter. "The physiological effects of a single one-hour session viewing a humorous video appear to last anywhere from 12 to 24 hours in different individuals," he reported.

Think about watching a funny movie today. Watch it tonight. Feel good for hours!

Good for a Laugh

The American Film Institute (AFI) shares the 100 funniest American films, as selected by a blue-ribbon panel of leaders from across the film community. Here are the top twenty-five from the list:

Some Like It Hot	Young Frankenstein
Tootsie	Bringing Up Baby
Dr. Strangelove Or: How I Learned to Stop Worrying and Love the Bomb	The Philadelphia Story
Annie Hall	Singin' in the Rain
Duck Soup	The Odd Couple
Blazing Saddles	The General
M*A*S*H	His Girl Friday
It Happened One Night	The Apartment
The Graduate	A Fish Called Wanda
Airplane!	Adam's Rib
The Producers	When Harry Met Sally
A Night at the Opera	Born Yesterday
	The Gold Rush

The New Horizons in Prevention

I have worked in the field of breast cancer since the 1970s and have witnessed phenomenal changes in the approach to breast cancer diagnosis, treatment, and survival. Surgical approaches, including breast conservation, were rare thirty years ago but are the norm today. Systemic therapy targeted to gene expression or protein markers on tumor cells for women who require adjuvant treatment, postdiagnosis, will produce better outcomes (reduce risk of recurrence) with fewer side effects. Currently, we rely on antihormonal therapies as a mainstay in endocrine-positive breast cancers, but newer therapies may have better tolerability with equal or better outcomes.

Natural products and lifestyle recommendations have been under investigation for years; the most powerful preventive we have seen to date targets lifestyle. It has been shown that increasing exercise and targeting a moderate weight are key factors that may reduce breast cancer risk. These factors also require constant practice, and the development of new skills and techniques, to help us keep moving and make healthy dietary choices.

~Carol Fabian, MD, breast medical oncologist at the University of Kansas Medical Center in Kansas City, where she directs the University of Kansas Cancer Center's Breast Cancer Prevention and Survivorship Centers

Are you searching for a medical provider to help you with questions about breast cancer prevention and survivorship?

- Do you wonder just how you will prevent breast cancer, hoping for a plan that will help you not get the disease like your family members?

- Do you have joint pain, fatigue, night sweats, lymphedema, osteoporosis, nausea, trouble with balance, sexuality issues, fatigue, neuropathy, depression, anxiety, and/or weight gain after treatment?

- Do you want a medical second opinion to address any side effects of your primary treatment (including, but not limited to, those above)?

- Do you have new questions weeks, months, or years after diagnosis?

- Do you want to know if new drugs or interventions have been developed to help prevent cancer from recurring or prevent new cancer from developing?

- Would you like access to a provider who understands your individual nutrition, exercise, mind-body needs, as they were affected by your cancer treatment?

- Do you want to be informed about the training in survivorship care of the medical provider you have chosen as a physician?

If you answered "yes" to any of the questions above, find a survivorship center or program near you at BackintheSwing.org. Wherever you go, ask for a personalized survivorship plan to optimize your health, just as you were given a plan for primary treatment. (See the resources page 240)

According to Jennifer Klemp, PhD, MPH, managing director of the Breast Cancer Survivorship Center at the University of Kansas Cancer Center, cancer survivorship care may be delivered in community oncology clinics or academic medical centers and may include physicians, nurse practitioners/physician assistants, psychologists, nurses, physical and occupational therapists, navigators, nutritionists, cardiologists, exercise physiologists, and support organizations.

This field is still emerging, as a result of the rapidly increasing number of survivors due to early detection and more effective treatments. There is an active movement to research survivorship care delivery models and to improve prevention and treatment options for the late and long-term effects of cancer.

~Jennifer Klemp, PhD, MPH, managing director of the Breast Cancer Survivorship Center at the University of Kansas Cancer Center

National Resources Focused on Survivorship Medical and Supportive Care Services

Organizations, websites, and other programs dedicated to helping you maintain lifelong wellness are ever changing, so we offer these listings below as examples of national pathways to learning and support for getting, and staying, back in the swing. Check with your medical providers and online sources for new online services, local health-related nonprofit organizations, community-based exercise and nutritional resources, and other lifestyle choices for getting, and staying, back in the swing.

AMERICAN CANCER SOCIETY

The American Cancer Society is the nationwide, community-based, voluntary health organization dedicated to eliminating cancer as a major health problem by preventing cancer, saving lives, and diminishing suffering from cancer, through research, education, advocacy, and service.

- 800-227-2345 or cancer.org

AMERICAN INSTITUTE FOR CANCER RESEARCH

The American Institute for Cancer Research funds research on the relationship of nutrition, physical activity, and weight management to cancer risk; interprets the accumulated scientific literature in the field; and educates people about choices they can make to reduce their chances of developing cancer.

- aicr.org

ANGIOGENESIS FOUNDATION

The Angiogenesis Foundation is dedicated to conquering disease using a new approach based on angiogenesis, the growth of new capillary blood vessels in the body, and positions itself as "the recognized, expert voice and champion of this new field of medicine."

- angio.org

BACK IN THE SWING USA®

Back in the Swing USA is a grassroots national nonprofit organization dedicated to improving and protecting well-being after breast cancer by supporting education for consumers and healthcare providers, and providing access to personalized, comprehensive survivorship clinical care.

- See page xi and BackintheSwing.org

BELLER NUTRITIONAL INSTITUTE

The Beller Nutritional Institute provides patients and the community with up-to-date information based upon leading-edge research concerning nutrition's impact on cancer prevention and treatment, heart disease, diabetes, and weight management. The message of the Beller Institute is simple and proactive: Disease prevention and recovery are intimately linked to nutritional intake and are more likely to be successful with informed and thoughtful nutritional support.

- bellernutritionalinstitute.com

BREAST CANCER RESEARCH FOUNDATION

The Breast Cancer Research Foundation's mission is to achieve prevention and a cure for breast cancer in our lifetime by providing critical funding for innovative clinical and translational research at leading medical centers worldwide, and increasing public awareness about good breast health.

- bcrfcure.org

CANCER SUPPORT COMMUNITY

The Wellness Community and Gilda's Club Worldwide joined forces to become the Cancer Support Community. The Cancer Support Community continues to optimize patient care by providing support groups, counseling, education, and healthy lifestyle programs.

- cancersupportcommunity.org

JOURNEY FORWARD

Journey Forward is a web-based program that helps cancer survivors know what they may have to face once their active treatment comes to an end.

- journeyforward.org

LANCE ARMSTRONG FOUNDATION

The Lance Armstrong Foundation is dedicated to inspiring and empowering people affected by cancer.

- laf.org

LIVING BEYOND BREAST CANCER

Living Beyond Breast Cancer is dedicated to empowering all women affected by breast cancer to live as long as possible with the best quality of life.

- Survivors' Helpline 888-753-LBBC (5222) or lbbc.org

METACANCER FOUNDATION

The MetaCancer Foundation provides resources and support for metastatic cancer survivors and their caregivers in everyday living, opportunities for creative reflection, and possibilities to live beyond the diagnosis with strength, grace, and peace.

- metacancer.org

NATIONAL CANCER INSTITUTE'S OFFICE OF CANCER SURVIVORSHIP

The Office of Cancer Survivorship strives to enhance the quality and length of survival of all persons diagnosed with cancer and to minimize or stabilize adverse effects experienced during cancer survivorship.

- 301-402-2964 or cancercontrol.cancer.gov/ocs/office-survivorship.html

NATIONAL COALITION FOR CANCER SURVIVORSHIP

The National Coalition for Cancer Survivorship is a survivor-led cancer advocacy organization whose members strive to ensure quality cancer care for all Americans and empower cancer survivors, caregivers, and clinicians.

- 888-650-9127 or canceradvocacy.org

SUSAN G. KOMEN FOR THE CURE

Susan G. Komen for the Cure funds research and community programs to save lives, empower people, ensure quality care for all, and energize science to find the cures to end breast cancer forever.

- komen.org

Y-ME

Y-ME National Breast Cancer Organization helps people find the information they need to make educated decisions. While they don't give medical advice, they do explain the information people are likely to encounter.

- 800-221-2141 for the YourShoes® 24/7 Breast Cancer Support Center

YOUNG SURVIVAL COALITION

Young Survival Coalition (YSC) is dedicated to critical issues unique to young women who are diagnosed with breast cancer, by offering resources, connections, and outreach so women feel supported, empowered, and hopeful.

- youngsurvival.org

Metric Conversions and Equivalents

METRIC CONVERSION FORMULAS

TO CONVERT	MULTIPLY
Ounces to grams	Ounces by 28.35
Pounds to kilograms . . .	Pounds by .454
Teaspoons to milliliters . .	Teaspoons by 4.93
Tablespoons to milliliters .	Tablespoons by 14.79
Fluid ounces to milliliters .	Fluid ounces by 29.57
Cups to milliliters	Cups by 236.59
Cups to liters	Cups by 0.236
Pints to liters	Pints by 0.473
Quarts to liters	Quarts by 0.946
Gallons to liters	Gallons by 3.785
Inches to centimeters . . .	Inches by 2.54

APPROXIMATE METRIC EQUIVALENTS

VOLUME

¼ teaspoon	1 milliliter
½ teaspoon	2.5 milliliters
¾ teaspoon	4 milliliters
1 teaspoon	5 milliliters
1¼ teaspoons	6 milliliters
1½ teaspoons	7.5 milliliters
1¾ teaspoons	8.5 milliliters
2 teaspoons	10 milliliters
1 tablespoon (½ fluid ounce)	15 milliliters
2 tablespoons (1 fluid ounce)	30 milliliters
¼ cup	60 milliliters
⅓ cup	80 milliliters
½ cup (4 fluid ounces) . . .	120 milliliters
⅔ cup	160 milliliters
¾ cup	180 milliliters
1 cup (8 fluid ounces) . . .	240 milliliters
1¼ cups	300 milliliters
1½ cups (12 fluid ounces) .	360 milliliters
1⅔ cups	400 milliliters
2 cups (1 pint)	460 milliliters
3 cups	700 milliliters
4 cups (1 quart)	0.95 liter
1 quart plus ¼ cup	1 liter
4 quarts (1 gallon)	3.8 liters

WEIGHT

¼ ounce	7 grams
½ ounce	14 grams
¾ ounce	21 grams
1 ounce	28 grams
1¼ ounces	35 grams
1½ ounces	42.5 grams
1⅔ ounces	45 grams
2 ounces	57 grams
3 ounces	85 grams
4 ounces (¼ pound)	113 grams
5 ounces	142 grams
6 ounces	170 grams
7 ounces	198 grams
8 ounces (½ pound)	227 grams

16 ounces (1 pound) . . . . 454 grams

35.25 ounces (2.2 pounds) . 1 kilogram

LENGTH

⅛ inch . . . . 3 millimeters

¼ inch . . . . 6 millimeters

½ inch . . . . 1¼ centimeters

1 inch . . . . 2½ centimeters

2 inches . . . . 5 centimeters

2½ inches . . . . 6 centimeters

4 inches . . . . 10 centimeters

5 inches . . . . 13 centimeters

6 inches . . . . 15¼ centimeters

12 inches (1 foot) . . . . . 30 centimeters

COMMON INGREDIENTS AND THEIR APPROXIMATE EQUIVALENTS

1 cup uncooked rice = 195 grams

1 cup all-purpose flour = 140 grams

1 stick butter (4 ounces • ½ cup • 8 tablespoons) = 110 grams

1 cup butter (8 ounces • 2 sticks • 16 tablespoons) = 220 grams

1 cup brown sugar, firmly packed = 225 grams

1 cup granulated sugar = 200 grams

OVEN TEMPERATURES

To convert Fahrenheit to Celsius, subtract 32 from Fahrenheit, multiply the result by 5, then divide by 9.

DESCRIPTION	FAHRENHEIT	CELSIUS	BRITISH GAS MARK
Very cool	200°	95°	0
Very cool	225°	110°	¼
Very cool	250°	120°	½
Cool	275°	135°	1
Cool	300°	150°	2
Warm	325°	165°	3
Moderate	350°	175°	4
Moderately hot	375°	190°	5
Fairly hot	400°	200°	6
Hot	425°	220°	7
Very hot	450°	230°	8
Very hot	475°	245°	9

Information compiled from a variety of sources, including *Recipes into Type* by Joan Whitman and Dolores Simon (Newton, MA: Biscuit Books, 2000); *The New Food Lover's Companion* by Sharon Tyler Herbst (Hauppauge, NY: Barron's, 1995); and *Rosemary Brown's Big Kitchen Instruction Book* (Kansas City, MO: Andrews McMeel, 1998).

Menu Planning Ideas

Holiday Theme

Make the holidays with family and friends a treat for you, too. Here are some of the dishes throughout the book that have a festive flair.

Fresh Ginger Cider **96**

Pomegranate Sparkler **91**

Orange-Cranberry Chutney **105**

Fresh Orange, Red Onion, and Pomegranate Salad **141**

Wilted Greens with Warm Cranberry Vinaigrette **142**

Festive Cider-Glazed Turkey Breast with Roasted Sweet Potatoes **218**

Roasted Spaghetti Squash with Tomatoes, Kale, and Herbs, vegetarian option **189**

Wild Rice and Cranberry Harvest Salad **158**

Orange-Glazed Carrots with Fresh Mint **163**

Roasted Apples and Squash with Rosemary **161**

Celebration Chocolate Cake **31**

Gingersnap-Crusted Pumpkin Pie **35**

Brunch

Many of these brunch foods can be made ahead of time; ask guests to bring a dish, and the whole meal can be a leisurely way to share the day.

Banana Flax-Jacks with Blackberry-Lavender Sauce **60**

Fall Harvest Waffles with Maple Syrup **62**

Retro Broiled Pink Grapefruit **53**

Blackberry-Lavender Compote **54**

Bellini-Style Peaches with Raspberries **51**

Lox of Love: Smoked Salmon with Bagels and Green Onion Cream Cheese **56**

Bountiful Breakfast Strata **66**

Wake-Up Pizza **68**

On the Go

One of the keys to Energy Balance is to keep from getting too hungry throughout the day, as hunger can trigger food choices you might not otherwise make. Including protein and whole carbohydrates (whole grains) will help. Planning for snacks while at work or on the road will help you prevent those impulse-buying decisions!

I'm Home and I'm Hungry! Dinner—Fast!

We've all experienced this—coming home and having to get dinner on the table before you or your family run over one another racing to the nearest cookie jar to satisfy those hunger pangs. Here are the quick-fix dishes that feed you well in a jiffy.

What's for Dinner?

Relax! Here is dinner, all figured out for you. Lots of choices and flavors to suit your fancy!

Caring and Sharing: Food to Comfort

It's always great to have a reliable stash of portable, potluck recipes to make and take to a gathering or to a friend in need of a little TLC. Many are remakes of favorite dishes—such as granola, broccoli-rice casserole, and carrot cake—that keep the essential flavor of the original dish, but give it a *Back in the Swing* twist.

Celebrate!

These dishes are great for parties and gatherings of all kinds, or when you feel like making a beautiful batch of glorious food and drink for you and your family to savor.

Acknowledgments

Only in growth, reform and change,
paradoxically, is true security to be found.

~Anne Morrow Lindbergh

No one deserves more thanks for planting the seeds of this book than the medical oncologists, nurses, social workers, and other health care professionals from around the world. They are the hub of the wheel of the clinical delivery of medical care that has become known as "survivorship care." Their dogged determination and singular focus—on the research, health care, and the advocacy sides of well-being—have resulted in today's ranks of over 2 million breast cancer survivors who are getting back in the swing of their lives every day.

Some of those caring practitioners have crossed our path, along our own journey, to grow the ranks of personalized comprehensive medical care that addresses preventing and resolving the effects of cancer treatment on the mind, body, and spirit. Others we have watched from afar. All have our admiration and respect for their partnership and mentoring: Karla Nichols, LSCSW; Jim Coster, MD; Charlene Wallace, RN, MS, OCN; Mary Callas, PT, DPT; Karin McCrary, RN; Moira Mulhern, PhD; Jane Murray, MD; Fran Jaeger

DrPH, MPH; Jennifer Klemp, PhD, MPH; Jenny Ling, OTR; Marty Thomas, MD; Vicki Meek, RN; Carol LaRue, OTR/L; Ellen Silver, LCSW; Ellen Heyman, MSN, RN, CS; Eileen Saffran, MSW; Jimmie Holland, MD; Katie Schmitz, PhD, MPH; Melinda Irwin, PhD MPH; Ellen Stovall; Patty Ganz, MD; Rachel Beller, MS, RD; Barbara Fredrickson, PhD; Vincent Cryns, MD; Deepak Chopra, MD; and David Simon, MD.

Our heartfelt gratitude to breast medical oncologist Carol Fabian, MD, medical director of the Breast Cancer Prevention Center and Survivorship Center at the University of Kansas Cancer Center, and her leadership team in medicine and nursing at the University of Kansas Hospital and Medical Center—Roy Jensen, MD; Barbara Atkinson, MD; Bob Page, Jeff Wright, and Cathy Glennon, RN, MHS, BC, CNA, OCN—who said "yes" early in our organization's history, when we proposed our vision for a Survivorship Center that would lead the nation in its multidisciplinary approach. The center's own research studies, funded by Back in the Swing, the National Cancer Institute, and others, inspired us to bring to light the results of literally hundreds of Energy Balance studies around the world—all focused on the clinical impact of nutrition and exercise, as well as lifestyle and environment, on reducing the risk of breast cancer and improving overall health and well-being.

Barbara treasures her friendship with Jennifer Klemp, PhD, MPH, who carefully reviewed this book's drafts and has been the guiding light of the Breast Cancer Survivorship Center at the University of Kansas Cancer Center, one of the first comprehensive centers of its kind in the country. Others who generously gave their time and talents to the development of this book include: Katy Harvey, MS, RD; Rachel Inoles, MS, RD; Catie Knight; Theresa Brown, PhD; Sarah Pressman, PhD; Mary Fry, PhD; Terese Babcock; Tracy Lunn; Marilyn Kelly; Linda Shalit; Louise Meyers; Vilma Subel; Jerry Wyckoff, PhD; Stan Johnston; Roz Varon; Donna Pelletier; Adele Hall; and Shawsie Branton. Thank you for demonstrating your enthusiasm for our mission with your thoughts, words, and deeds.

Our volunteer recipe consultants, Elaine Nelson and Ellen Katz, whom Barbara could never repay for their trusted companionship in all phases of her life, including this book, were champions of honesty about the fine details of each recipe. How lucky we are to have had their tasteful feedback.

The same holds true for Barbara's partner in business and in life, Bob Unell. Without his talented writing, editing, and researching skills, as well as his unconditional love and sense of humor, this book would not be sitting in your hands. Together with the enthusiastic cheerleading of their children, Amy Elizabeth and Justin Alex Unell, the impossible becomes possible.

Judith acknowledges the many people in her life who make meaningful projects like this possible: literary agent Lisa Ekus and a formidable army of tasters and testers, including Judith's culinary book club, friends, and family.

These dedicated community advocates of the Greater Kansas City Metropolitan Area—both Kansas and Missouri—deserve our admiration, as well, for being early adapters. They passionately embraced our mission of breast cancer survivorship over a decade before it was an established discipline in health care: Bill Hall; Laura McKnight; Neal Sharma; KO Strohbehn; Amie Jew, MD; Bob Regnier; Patrick McCarthy; Fran Brozman; Ed and Merry Prostic; Bill Patterson; Jane Rubenstein; Jill Raines; Jim and Jane Ferguson; Angie Ford; Suzi Blackman; Darcie Blake; Bev Chapman; Lon and Marcia Lane; Barclay Ross; Josh Hodapp; Tracey Kendall; and Jeff and Cathy Alpert are the frontline visionaries who believed unequivocally that we could accomplish our early goals. And we did, thanks to their friendship and faith. Every breast cancer survivor is better for your saying "yes."

The two leaders at Andrews McMeel Publishing and Universal UClick, respectively—Kirsty Melville and Lee Salem—must take full credit for their brilliant judgment that a book like this would be timely and trusted by everyone who has ever wondered if it would really be possible for her to get "back in the swing" and stay there after a diagnosis. Now everyone will have to wonder no more—thanks to the foresight of Kirsty and Lee—and can use this book to suit their own fancy. How much fun to join forces with their enthusiastic cohorts—Jean Lucas, Amy Worley, Lynne McAdoo, Sara Remington, Diane Marsh, Tammie Barker, Caty Neis, Erin Quon, Christine Wolheim, and Julie Barnes—who continue to

make good food, good health, and good times within the reach of each reader.

And finally, our gratitude to the volunteers, board of directors, sponsors, corporate partners, and retailers from around the country who work every day to make our focus of eating and living well the recipe for success of Back in the Swing USA. Thanks for the gifts of your time, treasure, and talents that keep us moving forward, appreciating the miracles of today and the promises of tomorrow.

Index